My Family Saga

Vera Turner

ISBN: 978-1-25708-079-3

PO Box 54 Datil, NM

Published by:

LULU Enterprises, Inc.
3101 Hillsborough Street
Raleigh, NC 27607
United States
www.lulu.com

Dedication

My granddad Amos Taylor was a constant in my life and he influenced my inner being. As a very small child I wanted to be favored by him. He walked home from work when we lived in the little houses near Steadman's Ord Ranch. I would spot him a long way down the driveway and would run to meet him. He always picked me up first because if he didn't he knew I would back off and pout.

When I got older, Granddad and I would work in the fields together. One day when we were picking up walnuts on the far corner of our twenty acre place, I was sitting on my bucket dropping an occasional walnut between my legs to hit the bucket. I told Granddad in a very slow serious tone, "Granddad, I think I am allergic to work."

He replied, "Is that what you call what you are doing?" He relayed this story at the dinner table many times. By his actions he was able to convey his strong work ethic and respect for others. The pioneer spirit and 'I can' attitude came through loud and clear and became an integral part of my being.

Granddad did the baby sitting when Mother and Daddy went out for a drive or to the movies. It was not a big difference because Granddad was always there. His chair was set up with his library table close at hand with his radio on it. He would let us kids listen to some of our favorite programs, but he had control and listened to the news and farm report. He also tuned in to the prize fights. Joe Louis is the only name I remember but he knew them all. I just made sure to get my reservation in for 'The Lone Ranger' and 'Straight Arrow'. We always had fun when Granddad was watching us because mainly he read and listened to the radio. As children my siblings and I were not entertained instead we were responsible for our own life.

March of 1966, Granddad was very ill. He had cancer in his mouth and throughout his digestive system. He had quit chewing tobacco years before but he still smoked his pipe. I was married and lived away from the ranch. When I visited it was sad to see him in the last stages of cancer. He had a sore throat all winter but didn't go to the doctor until early spring. He said, "They want to cut my tongue out so I can't talk."

It was too late for treatment. The last time I saw him was just days before he died. Mother had given him a towel to pull between his two hands because his hands moved constantly. He could barely speak and I was so sad I could hardly talk myself. He struggled to get out a few words.

"Just...like.....a.....cow"

I acknowledged that I heard what he said and he continued in a strained, struggling voice, "Sick.........all....winter........and.........die.........in.....the..........spring." He was making a joke to lighten the mood and help me to feel better. I had trouble talking but went to the kitchen to tell Mother what he had said and cried.

Granddad died at home and the doctor had to come to the house to pronounce him dead. The doctor's words to mother were, "He is truly the last of the Pioneers."

After Granddad's death he remained very close to me. All I had to do was think of him and he seemed to help me with any problem that I needed to solve. He was a constant comfort and encouragement to me.

In my life and raising my kids I had many challenges where he directed my response and actions. I was driving home to Sacramento from work one day in 1988 when he made his presence known. I didn't hear voices but it was a strong message directly to my brain. My Granddad told me I was OK and he was going to be with my premature grandson Leo. Leo had many challenges because he was born a drug addict and was premature. He was almost a year old and had very poor balance and his focus and attention were not developing properly. After my Granddad went to be close to him, his posture and development improved dramatically.

Granddad stayed close to Leo until July 28, 2009, when his baby girl was born prematurely. Granddad is watching over little Jorden Madison Jensen. I know she will be ok with her guardian angel watching over her.

This book covers all branches of my family tree but I would like to dedicate the book to my Granddad Amos Edgar Taylor.

About the author:
Vera Turner through the eyes of her
son Erik Albert Turner:

Sons tend to portray their mothers as maternal angels, casting their image through a lens of love and adulation showing one lovingly distorted image of who they really are. I happen to know my mom, so I will tell you about her. Vera is now a good friend of mine and although the most basic parts of our relationship really haven't changed all that much over the years I have recognized human aspects of her. My sisters and I know her for the strong matriarch she is, influencing the way many generations of our family will think and be. She'll always be present in us that she knows well and many she'll never know. I think that's important to her; she diligently works with all of us. Vera isn't interested in ruminating over what she has accomplished with herself and all of us, she is constantly thinking of the future. She knows it is within herself to have strong impact on those things she identifies as important. She has a pragmatic love for things; she sees a problem and solves it. Once Vera prioritizes an endeavor, she is ready to do whatever is required to make it a reality, she believes she can, can do, whatever it is that's important enough to spend time and attention on. I have seen her develop new ideas and redirect, but never quit or fail, two consequences that do not exist within her and she will always refute them as nonsense.

Curt and innovative she has been known to offend friends and occasionally family, although we have been conditioned for, and enjoy, this brazenness. Untempered and realistic without guilt for consequences, but paradoxically loving and filled with concern. When thrust into a new meeting Vera can be hard to understand and predict. I think she enjoys that and uses the misguided judgment of others, especially when diagnosing a problem. Inviting skepticism with her unorthodox ideas the following inevitable lack of understanding seems to give her private humor and fuel her fire at the same time; watch out for her first comment or reaction, beware if it strikes you as confusing, out of context or unreasonably harsh, just give her your attention, its what she's after and she'll get it sooner or later anyhow.

Vera is a 'HOW' we get this done, not an 'IF' we can get this done person. Like most lessons she's taught me, this one came by example. I bought my first truck at age seventeen with a loan attained with my mother's co-signature. After taking a corner too fast I was in the market for another loan and a new truck by age eighteen. Vera was less enthusiastic about the cosigning process a second time around. She took me to the Schools Federal Credit Union where the first loan was paid off via my insurance.

Fully aware this was a solo mission, I entered the bank by myself, unsure of whom I needed to talk to and very skeptical that I would be taken seriously. I exhausted all my mental resources to convince the loan officer that I was worthy of a loan in my name only. The story kept ending the same.

"We just need your mom to cosign again."

"She hates me." I lied.

So it was sheepishly back out to the car to give mom the news, knowing she would not accept my answer. So back in I went trying to sell the "She hates me" story as leverage to consummate a loan. Vera quickly tired of this merry-go-round and joined me for one more try. I figured when faced with the same stonewalling we could call it quits. The conversation with the loan officer unfolded in much the same manner, I thought we were done: I'm sure the young bank professional thought so as well.

That's when mom asked the question, "How do we get this done?" Now I know that it would only be fair to warn a person before they answered this question, but nothing could be done, so the inevitable, "we can't get this done" was the answer. Mom quickly retorted, "I asked HOW, can or can't isn't something I was wondering about." This invited an immediate private consultation between the young lady and her supervisor. She returned with renewed confidence that the answer was still "can't." After a feeble attempt to deny us, it became a negotiation between the supervisor and Vera. I think he realized quickly that his condescending tone and regurgitated loan requirement rules speech would not be sufficient to extinguish the situation he was faced with. In the end he extinguished the situation, my mother, by bending the rules and giving an auto loan in my name only. She was relentless until the percentage rate was also to her liking.

Like most sons at an early age, I at times thought she was insane and tried to thwart any interactions she had with my friends. The first time I realized the impact she could have on those struggling to learn and overcome came in a context where the results were tangible and important, the baseball diamond. She approached a teammate, Timothy Small, at least he was an outcast, this was a safe interaction and wouldn't disrupt my relentless pursuit of popularity. So I allowed the consultation, as though I had a choice.

We were amidst an endless practice after school on an extremely hot California afternoon, it was being elongated by a pitiful batter. Timothy had a knack for only swinging at pitches that were at least a foot out of the strike zone, usually pitches that were above his head. If by some miracle his bat touched the ball anything remotely close to a fair ball was played as such; it was law that every player must put the ball into play before practice was over. I crouched with my hands on my knees at shortstop bending my neck so that I could watch the birds flying above. With another slap of the ball in the catcher's mitt I knew that he had failed again. I looked over and saw that my mother had arrived to pick me up, practice was already late. I don't know how long she had been there, for all my bird identification, but she was intently watching every pitch and swing.

Eventually the pitcher threw a ball that sailed haphazardly into Timothy's bat, ricocheting into fair territory it dribbled past the pitchers mound and came to rest for a few seconds before I was aware that a ball was in play, with redemption in mind I put a little extra on a throw that overshot the first baseman into right field. After Timothy slid into second base and dusted himself off, practice was over. He headed to the dug out where my mother was waiting full of questions. I only remember one "Do you see the high pitches better? Are they easier to hit?"

Uninterested, I joined my friends across the diamond to point out what a fantastic baseball player I was, but took an occasional glance over to see what mom was up to. She had Timothy pointing and swinging at things. Still oblivious of her project I started playing with my friends, meanwhile a half hour of personal tutoring was simultaneously transpiring.

Mom called for me and we headed home. "That boy was swinging at the wrong ball," she glibly stated. "Tell me how Timothy bats tomorrow; I want to know if he makes a field goal."

"A base hit mom, its baseball!"

"Tell me if he swings the bat and connects with the ball easier tomorrow."

"Whatever mom."

The next day was the first time Timothy ever made consistent contact with the ball, he no longer dreaded stepping up to the plate and although he was still a hapless baseball player, Mom shaved a good half hour off practice everyday.

I learned later that Vera recognized Timothy had double vision, he was swinging at the wrong ball when it was in certain areas, the strike zone being one! When the ball came at his waist he swung the bat uselessly above his head, we had always wondered why he could only hit a ball pitched high in the air.

Perhaps the most profound effect of Timothy's new found hand eye coordination came weeks later when the school bully began picking on him again. Timothy instructed his friends how to work with him as my mother had, placing targets with their hands in different locations as he adjusted for the effects of his vision, beaming and excited while he moved increasingly fast, ending the practice sessions confident. The next confrontation started familiar enough as the barrel chested bully tried dragging Timothy to the ground, but this time the much slighter boy sent cascading punches connecting in a painfully frequent fashion. Stunned and bloodied the bully didn't seem to need anything else with Timothy.

Mom never backs down from a fight or a challenge, there have been dozens of Timothy Small's over the years, many times myself. Her relentless "I can" attitude is more prevalent now that she has written the book about her family history. Vera remains uninterested in letting things be. She is always teaching, healing and campaigning looking only toward the future.   By: Erik Albert Turner

Granddad Amos Edgar Taylor holding eighteen month old Vera. In 1942 this picture was taken on the first property the Wilks family bought in California.

Daddy Elbert William Wilks standing beside ten year old Vera. This picture was taken Easter Sunday in the side yard at the ranch house in 1950.

Table of Contents

Introduction to My Family Saga
by Vera Turner

A family saga dedicated to my Granddad Taylor. Where did the strong willed nature and the confidence to make decisions come from? I just thought everyone had these problem solving abilities. The people around me had these traits and when I looked at my lineage I found lots of strong wills and self sufficient people with a persistent and dedicated way of operating.

My Dad and Mother made their way to California and started a whole new life just like the ancestors made their moves from England to the new world. Other groups that formed my lineage made their own trips. The Harts moved from Indiana to Weatherford, Texas and the Wilks/Davis/Evans groups came from Oak Grove, Limestone county, Alabama to Texas. Granddad Taylor was the leader in his family but in his older years he lived quietly with his daughter Vona and son-in-law Elbert Wilks.

Decisions that I made were valued by my family so I just grew up making decisions. My Dad always said, "the only way to fail is not to try" so when things didn't work out the way I planned I knew that I just needed to learn from the situation and redirect with a new set of decisions to accomplish the goal. I was grown before I was told that I was making decisions. I just thought it was the way to live.

I was commended in my profession because I had to organize programs that were just being funded. I didn't have a model to follow and the funding and staffing would change so I would have to look at all the parameters and reorganize often. This is not a problem for me. The 'I can' attitude is in full force solving any need.

I worked with the brain storming sessions of the Galt Community Mental Health Clinic established in the late 1970s. This was a great project for me because the organization and outreach ideas came quickly and we had talented staff to carry out the ideas. It was more challenging as the funding was shrinking. During this period a group from UC Davis was doing a study of the activists in the community, and I was one they interviewed. They wanted to identify the source of the ideas and the nature of active community organizers.

One question I remember the lady asking, "How do you deal with failure?"

My quick reply, "I don't fail" surprised the interviewer. This stopped the interview and then she had to explain what she was trying to find out so I told her how I looked at every situation and the only way you FAIL is if you stop before a solution is found. I am quick to redirect and reevaluate to arrive at a satisfactory conclusion. "I CAN'T never did anything," was imprinted in my head. So CAN'T is not an option. The interview with the researcher enlightened me to characteristics in myself that direct my life. These attributes didn't just happen. I know my Granddad's approach to life came through to me directly and by way of my Mother and Dad.

The struggles and different paths that converged to create my ancestry is a good story. I will relate the highlights in my matter of fact style with many side stories that I have heard and some of the historical stage.

Part I
New Mexico to New Mexico

John Hart married Mahala Niblack
and begat **Joseph Hart**
Robert C. Hart
others
Joseph Hart married Elizabeth Sharpe
and begat George
John A. Hart
Joseph Hart later married Susan C. Walden
and begat **Mahala Elizabeth (Bettie)**
Joseph J. Hart
Tom Hart
7 others
Robert Taylor married **Mahala Elizabeth (Bettie) Hart**
and begat **Amos Edgar Taylor**
Leslie Taylor
Leroy Taylor
Plez Taylor
Tinna Taylor
Emma Taylor
Maude Taylor
Kate Taylor
Amos Edgar Taylor married Timpie Leolin Southerland
and begat Everett Perry Taylor
Vera B. Taylor
John Lee Taylor
James Owen Taylor
Vona LaVoyce Taylor (Wilks, Wilson)

This family saga is dedicated to my Granddad Taylor. Hart is the little town where Granddad grew up and Hart is his family name. This region was Indian Territory when Granddad's grandparents arrived. Joseph and Susan Hart settled in this community soon after their marriage. Hart officially became a town when my Great Uncle Joseph J Hart established a Post Office by that name. Much later, Hart, Indian Territory became the state of Oklahoma on November 16, 1907.

Joseph and Susan Hart

Hart, Oklahoma

At age sixteen my Granddad Taylor lived in Hart and was affectionately referred to as 'Old Man Taylor' by town folk. He also had the nickname of 'Aim' and the name 'Aim' stayed with him until his death March 13, 1966. He was my grandfather, Amos Edgar Taylor, born in Bonham, Texas, November 26, 1882. He was one of many children in the family of Robert Taylor and Mahala Elizabeth Hart Taylor (later known as Bettie Patton). When his dad died in 1901 he took over responsibility for the family and worked to put the other siblings through school.

A neighbor, John Henry Southerland, liked Aim because he was a hard worker. Mr. Southerland had a house full of girls and only one boy so he often hired Aim. His girls were known all over the county as the prettiest girls around. Mr. Southerland traveled as a Justice of the Peace and in one photo he is shown on the steps of the court house in a Vigilante group. While he traveled around, his wife Sally and the girls took care of the farm. His oldest daughter Timpie Leolin was in school when Aim was attending school events with his siblings and helping at the Southerland farm. The 1900 census shows a well populated community and in about 1902 a picture of Hart School shows over seventy students in attendance.

Timpie Leolin Southerland in Hart School

There is a pretty girl named Timpie Leolin Southerland in the third row from the top and three from the left. She has her hair pulled up with a roll in the front. Timpie's high white collar is accented with a ruffled bodice. Howard, her older brother and four sisters are in the picture. I don't know which ones are Granddad's siblings, but I know they are in the picture also.

The Southerland's lived in Hart, Indian Territory since January 1894 when their daughter Annie was born. Timpie and other Southerland children were born in Texas where John Henry and Sally Edna Traylor met near Cooksville, Titus County, Texas. Sally's brother Jim had descendants still living in Daingerfield and Cooksville area when Vona, my mother, and I visited in 1995.

After Robert Taylor's death at the age of fifty on February 4, 1901, Aim's mother, Bettie, remarried and became a Patton. Mr. Patton was not good to the younger kids so he didn't stay in the family very long. The Pattons were from Clarita.

Living in Indian Territory, Aim faced hardships and death. The siblings that Aim raised and put through school were a real joy to him. He saw to it that the younger kids got to school, to social events, and a good start in life.

Tinna and Emma, two of his beautiful sisters, became telephone operators in Sherman, Texas. Plez, one brother, was a 'sharp shooter' in the army during WW1 and rode on a train to different stations as advertisement for the war. Maude and Kate were in Tupelo, Oklahoma, but they died young and neither had a family. Brothers Lee Roy and Leslie were married and had families. Aim married Timpie Leolin Southerland on July 10, 1904, not realizing that they only had fourteen years to be together. By the time Aim was twenty-four they had a baby boy named Everett Perry. A daughter, Vera B. Taylor was born August 19, 1907. The Taylor family moved to a number of small communities in a fifty mile radius of Hart. They would rent a place to grow cotton as a money crop and grain for the animals.

During my visit in 1978, I asked why they moved so often, Pete Taylor answered, "The ground would wear out and they didn't use fertilizer in those days."

4

Eventually, Aim's brothers Lee Roy and Leslie settled with their families near Clarita. Aim and Timpie moved down by the creek near Clarita. They were working hard to make a living for their young family. Granddad told me the story of shooting wood rats and skinning them so Timpie would not know that they were rats. Timpie made a great tasting squirrel stew and never was the wiser. Or at least she didn't let Aim know if she knew. Timpie kept a neat, clean cabin and Aim took care of the animals. His mules were a big help when it was time to plow. Aim brought in the water for Timpie to use in the kitchen. She was a good cook and Aim always had a big breakfast. He loved his coffee strong, bacon and eggs, and biscuits with red eye gravy (gravy thinned with coffee).

After breakfast, he would hitch the team and lead them to the field. He then strapped the lead around himself and took hold of the plow and started around the outside edge of the field. A quarter section (160 acres) was a big area to walk behind a single blade plow. As soon as the rounds allowed turn around room at each end, he would turn at the end of each row and double back. The single blade plow threw up just enough soil for a planting hill and the furrow was deep enough to catch any water that fell. Dry land farming was a gamble and plenty of work. He walked around the field and back and forth, the second time to plant. Over the field another time to thin and pull weeds. Many times around so the crop could be planted, tended, picked and cleared. Patience and perseverance were a must to start tilling 160 acres behind a single blade plow each year.

One day, Aim came in to the cabin tired from plowing and sat down. He watched Timpie working on a huge tablecloth with a fine crochet hook. She said, "I don't know how you have the patience to work that big field with such a little plow."

Aim replied, "I guess the same way you go around a huge table cloth with such a tiny needle." They just chuckled as they thought about the comparison. This is a memory that my granddad related to me thirty-five years after Timpie's death.

Wagon Train to New Mexico

Aim's brothers Lee Roy and Leslie had families of their own living in Eastern Oklahoma when the doctor diagnosed both of them with Tuberculosis. Consumption it was called earlier, but in those days they called it TB. Doctors had a prescription for it. Move to New Mexico or death. Cora, Leslie Taylor's wife, had a sister already living in Estancia, NM, area. A.B. McKinley, a family acquaintance, had also taken his ailing wife to New Mexico. Uncle Tom and Josephine Hart with their children Les, Jasper, Claude and Elbert were in New Mexico for the same reason.

Mollie, Lee Roy Taylor's wife, wanted to have a little more time with her family together. Their five children, Bill, Irene, Lona May, Pete and the baby Victor made for a wagon full on the trip to New Mexico. Mollie and Lee Roy needed help and so did Cora, Leslie, and their daughter. The brothers wanted my Granddad to go with them, because they knew they didn't have long to live.

Aim and Timpie had been married three years and had Everett and an infant girl Vera B. Aim didn't want to go, but when the brothers said they were going with or without him, responsible Aim loaded his family in a wagon and joined the other two families heading for New Mexico.

The journey was long, crowded and too strenuous for Lee Roy who was the sickest of the two. Just a few days out Lee Roy and Mollie were put on the train to finish the journey. Cora's sister and Tom and Josephine Hart were already near Estancia and they helped on that end of the journey. Aim, Timpie, and Cora brought the Taylor caravan into Estancia and they took out a homestead between Tijique and Torreon due west of Estancia. Aim, the kids, and wives dug the half-dugout homes.

The Taylor's settled about three miles from A.B. McKinley who had just lost his wife. McKinley was logging and had sawmills in the Manzano mountains to the west which provided Aim with work. He was the only able bodied man in the group. The families lived in half-dugouts. The dugout part of the structure made half the wall and a tent was used for the roof. Other homesteaders that stayed built wooden upper parts. The air was dry but very cold.

Life in New Mexico was challenging. Aim worked six days a week with his two mules Tony and Kate dragging logs out of the mountains and into a clearing. In camp he had the task of chopping shingles. He could split off a cedar shingle with one blow of the ax. On Sunday, he would walk home to be with his son Everett, his baby girl Vera B. and wife Timpie. He was often asked why he didn't ride home in the wagon. His quick reply was always the same, "My mules need a day of rest."

Vera B. was a cute, vivacious baby and would run to meet her daddy when he came home from the woods until she suffered from infantile paralysis. It was painful to see the effects of the disease on his little girl. He didn't speak of her often, but he did comment about how close her birth date was to mine. She was born on August 19th and my birth date is August 18th. Vera B. died on March 24, 1909 before she turned two years old and is buried in the Estancia Cemetery near Estancia, New Mexico. She laid there for almost ninety years without a proper marker. In front of the brick for baby Taylor is a new tombstone giving tribute to her short life. Her sister, Vona LaVoyce Taylor Wilks Wilson, had the marker installed in 1997. I thank Vera B. for my name.

When I was writing this book and living in New Mexico, I met relatives of Cora. One of my friends overheard a discussion about Cora and she joined in because Cora was the cook at the hospital when her son was born. Carolyn Wells lived in Claunch, New Mexico, and she remembered how hungry she was after her son was born. Word got back to Cora in the cafeteria, so she made an extra dinner for Carolyn and brought it to her room. She said, "The hospital dinners are not enough for farm girls like us." This is a kindness long remembered.

Dry land farming was sweeping the country in the early 1900's and beans were being raised in the arid country around Estancia. The railroad came through Mountainaire and the towns were booming. A. B. McKinley found the Fourth of July Springs and hosted a picnic for the entire community each Independence Day. This location is now preserved as a portion of the Cibola National Forest and the only spot in New Mexico where the Crimson Maple tree grows. The Fourth of July Spring feeds the Tijique Creek where Aim and A.B. McKinley had their logging camp. Plenty of wild turkeys made a quick meal for the crew.

Cora's husband, Leslie Taylor, my grandfather's brother, died March 27, 1908. After his death, Cora worked for A.B. McKinley and helped him with his young boys he had to raise after his wife died. Cora married A.B. McKinley on March 19, 1909, and stayed in New Mexico tending the graves of her first husband, a child that died shortly after Leslie and the family my granddad left behind.

Aim's other brother Lee Roy died March 16, 1909. Days later Vera B. died. Aim wanted to leave New Mexico and get the families back to Oklahoma. Uncle Tom Hart was still living, but he was very sick. My Granddad loaded up his family and Aunt Mollie, Lee Roy's widow, and her kids for the ride back to Eastern Oklahoma. They were joined by ailing Tom Hart, Aunt Josie, and family. Cora's family stayed near Estancia.

Leaving behind his two brothers and his precious little girl Vera B. was just another painful 'must' in Amos Edgar Taylor's life. This hurtful chapter is well marked in the Estancia Cemetery. In 1957, when Granddad took a trip through New Mexico he was within thirty miles of Estancia and just neglected to mention anything about that period in his life.

Aim, again the only able bodied man in a wagon train of ladies, children, and his very ill Uncle Tom Hart, sent word ahead to his cousin John Wesley Hart and friend George Warren so they could meet them and help with the return. Later, John Wesley Hart married Mary Ellen Admire Taylor (Aunt Mollie) and George Warren married Josephine Hart after Tom died in Oklahoma.

When Aim returned to Oklahoma, he had no home place so he took his family to stay with Timpie's parents John Henry and Sally Edna Southerland in Hart, Oklahoma. Granddad pulled cotton bolls until his fingers bled, but he made enough money to get relocated near Clarita, Oklahoma.

The Roff Newspaper of 1909 has articles of the Southerland and Taylor families and Arthur Hart, Uncle Joe's boy is also mentioned.

'Aug. 27, 1909, Amos Taylor and family came in from New Mexico on Monday and are visiting Mrs. Taylor's parents, J.H. Southerland and wife this week. Jim (this is Sally Southerland's brother) *says it is too dry for him. They went there last November.'* *'September 3, 1909, H.O. Southerland* (Howard is Timpie's brother) *came in Sunday from Francis, where he has been teaching school. He has dismissed his school until the first of November on account of the students having to pick cotton.' 'December 31st 1909, Mrs. Amos Taylor of the Choctaw country, is visiting her parents, Mr. and Mrs. J.H. Southerland.'*

Choctaw Country is the area around Clarita. Bill Taylor, one of Aunt Mollie and Lee Roy Taylor's boys, married a Choctaw Princess named Martha. Aunt Mollie's children Irene, Bill, Lona May, and Pete Taylor were cousins of my mother. Pete and Lona were tour guides in 1978 for Vona and I when we visited Roff, Hart, Frisco, and Clarita.

**Lona May and Vona by Timpie's headstone in
Moore Cemetery near Clarita, Oklahoma (taken in 1978)**

Lona May Taylor Davidson had a new house built on the spot where Aunt Mollie's house had been. Mother had many memories of riding the train and the engineer putting her off in the back pasture, so she could walk up to Aunt Mollie's house. The Colored lady that lived on the hill the other way made big sugar cookies for the kids. Mother always loved to visit her. Sadly, her son was hanged when he was in high school. Supposedly, looked at a white girl. These memories were all after Timpie had died and Mother lived near Frisco. A short train ride took Vona to Aunt Mollie's house.

After the cotton was in, Aim and Timpie had a nest egg from Aim's long days of cotton picking. They moved back to Clarita and made preparation for the next year. Granddad had to shock enough wild grain for the animals to feed on during the winter. It took a number of sheaves of grain to make enough upright stacks to feed the mules until spring grass came up. The cousin John Wesley Hart lived close by and helped Aunt Mollie relocate and soon married her.

My Uncle Lee was born and named John Lee Taylor on February 13, 1911. Five year old Everett Perry was there to welcome his new brother. James Owen, another baby boy was born in 1913, but died just months later. Ten year old Everett and five year old Lee welcomed a baby sister on April 13, 1916. My mother Vona LaVoyce was born in the little cabin by the creek. It was actually in Clarita but Coalgate was listed as her official place of birth.

This cabin had a screened in front porch where the cousins could sleep when they got together. The families and friends worked together to help each other. The Patton's were from this area so when Aim's mother Bettie Taylor remarried she moved to Clarita. Mr. Patton was not good to the children so Bettie lived on her own and moved to Madill, Oklahoma, where she efficiently ran a boarding house. She earned her own way by running the boarding house with the help of her two daughters Emma and Tinna. Sunday dinners were a specialty and brought in towns people just to have a good meal.

Aim's young sisters Emma and Tinna moved across the state line to Sherman, Texas, and became telephone operators. Emma and Tinna were close enough to visit their mother in Madill. When Emma got sick, she went to live with her mother Bettie Patton. The hometown doctor didn't believe in using the knife even though he knew she had appendicitis. By the time her brother Aim arrived and quickly decided she needed an operation it was too late. In the wagon on the way to the hospital in Sherman, Texas, Emma died May 29, 1918, from a ruptured appendix.

Later that year, Tinna had meningitis. Aim just happened to visit Tinna. Since she wasn't at work he went to the home where she lived with another family. The family had left Tinna at home knowing she didn't feel well, but they had no idea how much pain was in store.

When Aim arrived he heard banging on the walls. He broke in to find Tinna out of her head in pain. She was throwing her body against the walls. It took six men to hold her down to give her medication for the pain. Mayo Clinic doctors treated her at the Sherman Texas Hospital. She made an apparent recovery from the meningitis when she developed another condition which resulted in a swollen abdomen. Aim helped his mother Bettie Patton care for Tinna and suffered with her as the pain increased and finally claimed her life on November 4, 1918, less than a month after Timpie's death.

Both sisters are buried in Madill, Oklahoma, with Woodsman tombstones. The headstones are shaped like a tall tree stump and they tower above others on the lonely hillside of the Madill Cemetery.

Before the 1918 flu swept the country, Amos E. and Timpie Taylor lived in the community of Clarita with their three remaining children Everett twelve years old, Lee seven, and Vona two. Aim farmed, hunted and fished. He was raised in real pioneer days when hunting and fishing were a necessity rather than a sport. Timpie Leolin's mother Sally Edna Southerland was a short, Dutch-German lady and a skilled midwife, so Timpie was well versed in caring for the sick. My grandparents, the caretakers, were busy during the flu epidemic of 1918.

Aim and Timpie traveled with team and buggy to many homes. Rubbing alcohol, aspirin, Minit Rub, and mustard plasters were the remedies. Comforting the sick with a damp cloth to bring down the fever and trying to get the patients to take some broth was about all that could be done.

Timpie treated the patients and Aim did the milking, feeding and any chores that needed to be done. Most people were afraid to go near the flu because too many were dying. Neighbors tried to talk Aim and Timpie out of going to help the flu victims. Aim and Timpie continued to care for the sick, traveling at night and staying to be with dying flu victims, until they themselves became helpless with the flu. Timpie's sisters and mother came to care for them. October 19, 1918, Timpie was getting better, Aim was still out of his head with fever. The first day that Timpie could sit up, she died from the exertion.

Assuming that Aim would die soon, the family buried Timpie in the Moore Cemetery and distributed the children among relatives. Everett, Lee, and Vona (just two years old) were to be cared for by Timpie's sisters.

Days later when Aim recovered he was horrified to find that his kids had been given away and his wife was dead and buried. He gathered his kids and raised them alone. My mother Vona was raised by her father and she carried on the 'I CAN' attitude when she at the age of 38 had to take on a farming operation and raise four children after the death of her husband.

In 1918, days after Amos Edgar Taylor recovered from the flu, he went to Madill, Oklahoma, to care for his sister Tinna that died Nov. 4, 1918. Granddad always said, "People must take time to bury their dead. When they get too busy for this the human race is in trouble."

Aim had experienced the grim reminders of the temporary nature of life which puts life in a different perspective. Amos Edgar Taylor was a determined, stoic person that could make a decision and take care of anything. I never heard my Grandfather speak a harsh word. He was loved and respected by all. He was always helpful in the community but some said he was too easy on Vona. He never made her work in the field but his work ethic was a part of my mother's being and she raised four kids with the same 'I can' attitude and a strong work ethic.

Aim finished the 1919 crop near Clarita where he raised cotton. In the early 1920's he moved his family, herd of cows, and farming equipment to the ranch headquarters owned by Garland Bab--near Frisco, Oklahoma. The big house was built on a knoll (old Indian burial ground) overlooking the creek bottom. There was a row of out buildings that included a tack room, seed house, smokehouse, and barn. The well was used by surrounding farms in drought seasons. This deep water well was just out the back door with a big tree beside it. Cotton was the money crop and corn was raised for the animals. The meadows were stacked with shocks of wild grass to feed the cows.

Garland Bab was a wealthy rancher who didn't mind throwing his weight around in the community. He was married to a Native American and had two boys called Pick and Bill. When Aim rented the ranch house Garland moved down the hill into a beautiful new home. Lee and Everett went to school with Pick and Bill Bab. Aim had help moving his herd. Two riders were hired to drive the cattle. The wagon was loaded with household items. The first night out they camped on the Boggy (big bridge wasn't built yet). The riders drove the cattle across the creek while my Granddad started the camp fire and was brewing a pot of coffee. Vona was sitting around keeping warm when she was startled by the riders coming up the creek. This was an exciting move for a little girl not quite four years old that had lost her mother just a little over a year ago.

Vona remembered both of her grandmothers living at the two story ranch house. Great-grandma Hart was born in 1840 so she was in her 80's. Vona remembers her around the kitchen helping, but she didn't do the heavy work like bringing in the water or tending the ash frame to make the lye to use in making soap. In her day she had done it all, but now she had help! Grandma Hart was a little forgetful and was constantly looking for her glasses or her pipe. Now she had plenty of time to sit by the fire and read or smoke her corn cob pipe.

**Aunt Fannie Noggles, Bettie Patton, Susan Hart
helped Aim with the family after Timpie died**

Vona about 4 years old

Grandmother Bettie Patton moved in after her financial crisis. One afternoon Bettie deposited $3,000 in the bank only to have it close with her life savings and operating money. Bettie was needed to help care for her mother and motherless grandchildren so she moved in with Aim.

Taking care of Vona was not always easy. Vona couldn't remember what she had done but, "Grandma Patton raked me out from under the seed house with a hoe."

Bettie died October 4, 1921, and was buried in the Frisco Cemetery. Vona was told by her dad to stand beside Greatgrandma Hart's chair. Aim had unloaded Grandma Hart and her chair from the wagon for the graveside services of her daughter Mahala Elizabeth Hart Taylor Patton.

Susan C. Hart had outlived her husband Joseph P. and all but one of her children. Uncle Joe came by to see his mother while she lived with Aim, Everett, Lee and Vona. Uncle Joe was a most colorful character, but I never met him. He would write interesting, poetic letters to Vona in Gridley, California, in later years when he was living in Colorado.

Uncle Joe was always a story teller. Vona remembered evenings with Uncle Joe, storytelling as entertainment, lying in the yard and chasing fire flies. The Indian burial mound in the front yard was the setting for the ghost stories that he would tell to the children. The stories often times were about his half-brothers John and George that came into Weatherford, Texas, with their grandmother Mahala Hart.

The half-brothers were noted for playing tricks on anyone they could catch in a prank. John A. Hart is even published with one chapter devoted to pranks and mischief that he and George pulled on others. Uncle Joe followed in their footsteps by kidding and scaring the kids.

One story that he related was how they would squirt milk at each other directly from the cows teats. All enjoyed the visits from Uncle Joe. One time Albert, Uncle Joe's son, came in his Model T Ford and Vona remembered vividly getting her fingers stuck in the door handle. Albert was showing off his new car by driving around and around in the yard.

My Granddad, Uncle Aim to some, has always been a gentle but strict disciplinarian. He was generous and helpful to many throughout his life. A friend Ely Baitey from Ada, Oklahoma, was widowed and had a son that was getting out of hand. Ely came to Aim with a proposition.

"Please take this teenage boy and try to make something out of him."

"That will be a tall order but I'll try," said Aim. Lee Baitey was into everything and respected nothing.

The tall tree standing in the yard had an adult swing in it. The ropes were long and about an inch in diameter. The bottom was a flat board. Uncle Joe, Lee and Everett, and Granddad enjoyed the swing. Vona was too little, but she watched as adults and big kids were swinging.

The branch above the swing had a nest of fledglings. Naturally, Lee Baitey was attracted by the possibility of robbing the nest. Why? Who knows? Probably just to say he did it. Granddad caught him as he had nearly accomplished his dirty deed. Granddad had warned him earlier to leave the nest alone and this defiance was not tolerated.

A little buck shot helped Lee Baitey get the message and he was in such a hurry to get down from the nest that he came down the rope of the swing. His hands were so rope burned that he spent the next few weeks doctoring his hands. He had to take care of them himself because he got no sympathy from Aim. This confrontation helped a teenage rebel grow up in a hurry. Later, we hear from Ely and Lee Baitey in Uncle Lee's journal so I know they stayed in touch.

By 1922, Susan C. Walden Hart was getting up in years and needed constant care so Aim propped her in the bed of a wagon and took her to Aunt Mollie's house in Clarita, Oklahoma. On the way out, three men came riding toward the wagon. They were not real friendly and looked like they were up to no good.

As they approached one man asked, "Are you leaving?"

Aim gave a short answer with no explanation, "Yep." The riders rode on toward Aim's farm. Aim clicked the reins and on they rattled across the Boggy toward Clarita. Mollie, the sister-in-law that Aim brought back from New Mexico, had her new husband John Wesley Hart and children Bill, Irene, Pete, Lona May and new baby Audie at home, but she took care of Grandma Hart until her death in 1926 at the age of 86.

Pete Taylor remembered the years that Grandma Hart spent at his house. He became a teenager and the radio was a novelty. When they played the radio Grandma Hart would yell, "Who's there?"

The radio couldn't answer so she would call again, "Who's there?"

No amount of explaining helped Grandma Hart understand that the voice was coming out of a box. She continued to ask, "Who's there?" when the radio was talking.

Mollie kept Grandma Hart propped up in bed with beautiful bolster pillows. She was cared for and life was made easy the last few years. Aim and his kids visited Aunt Mollie and Grandma Hart on occasion.

Naturally, the big sugar cookies that the Negro lady on the hill made were the clearest memories. There was a railroad station in Frisco and the engineer would let Vona off in the field behind Aunt Mollie's so she could visit often. Dr. Truax was the local doctor and the family Mr. and Mrs. Pigg ran the store near the train station. They had a seat swing in the back yard and would give Vona a drink. She had an open account at the store so she could buy candy and snacks.

"Yep," they were leaving to take Grandma Hart to Clarita but Aim and Vona returned to their farm a few days later. The mysterious riders had been busy poisoning the well.

Lee and Everett had stayed behind to take care of the pigs and cattle when Aim and Vona took Grandma Hart to stay with Aunt Mollie. Lucky for them they did not do a good job. They forgot to water the animals and they were off visiting Pick and Bill Bab. When my Granddad pulled in the yard, he knew something was wrong. The animals were thirsty and when he started to let down the well bucket he complained, "Those boys have been playing with chalk around here."

Aim kept at his work and got the water to the stock. The pigs were the first to get sick. A neighbor and friend came by and had coffee with my Granddad. The fellow got real sick so he came back to check on the family. When the boys got home Aim, Vona, and the animals were all sick.

Aim was sick, but he went out and checked the "chalk" around the well. It was arsenic and the boys certainly had not put it there. Aim sent for help down to Garland Bab's and went to work combating the arsenic with milk. Garland Bab did have enemies all over the area so when they thought Aim Taylor was leaving they were going to get Garland.

Actually, Aim was the one that got hurt. Timpie's folks in Hart took in the family until they were better from the poisoning. Shortly, Aim and family were well enough to return to a nearby farm. I visited the farm with Vona, Pete, and Lona May in 1978. The barn was still standing, so I got a picture of the barn with a rusty roof. You cross the 'big' bridge and then around the corner is the barn on the right hand side of the road.

Granddad's barn just over the big bridge

'Big 'Bridge

**Pete, Lona, Vona by Bettie Patton's grave in Frisco,
Oklahoma cemetery**

Joseph P. Hart, Susan's husband had died in 1898 when they lived in Hart, Indian Territory. Aunt Mollie's son Pete Taylor took me to see the cemetery in 1978. Outside of Frisco we looked for the cemetery where Bettie Patton was buried. Pete couldn't tell which way to go to the cemetery because of all the changes in the roads and lay of the land. When I saw the direction sign to Frisco Cemetery he said, "Well I guess they moved the cemetery." Mother remembered standing beside Grandma Hart at the cemetery so she was the one who located Bettie Patton's grave.

Then we drove on to Roff and the roads were under construction, so Pete Taylor walked over to a little store and talked to some locals. Following their directions we drove through the construction area and then walked a creek bank to get to Hart Cemetery where Joseph P. Hart is buried with a prominent marker. The creek circled around a grove of oak trees on a knoll. The cemetery was typical of places Granddad had lived--a knoll overlooking a creek.

Near Frisco, Oklahoma, close to the Big Boggy, Aim raised three kids on his own. Aim recalled the time he almost drowned Vona. She was with him plowing in the field when a down pour started. Aim unhitched Tony and Kate, picked up Vona like a sack of potatoes, and ran to the house leading the team and carrying Vona under his arm. Her face was turned toward the rain and she was turning blue when they reached the house.

Mother often spent time at the house alone and Granddad had it set up so she could fix something to eat. He always had jars of peanut butter and jelly, crackers and bread, and pickles on the table for snacks. If dark fell before Aim got home, Vona would go outside and sit in a tree to wait for her Dad, because she didn't want to be alone in the house.

Everett, the oldest brother, was the organizer of the house and helped with the ironing, mending, and taught Vona how to write her name. Mother kept the iron that Everett whittled a new handle for when he was responsible for the house.

Uncle Lee and mother were closer together in age. Mother was just five years younger than Lee so they did more arguing and competitive play. Lee always wanted Vona to walk to school by herself so he could be with his friends. Vona had to cross Boggy Creek on the way to school, but her brother Lee didn't care and he would ditch her and make her walk alone.

Everett was ten years older than Vona and he took care of Vona and chores around the house. Aim had made him stay in school until he finished eighth grade, but he was helping around the farm when Vona started to school.

It was during this first grade year that Vona watched the 'big' bridge being built. Driving across the bridge in 1978 we got a big laugh about how little it really was. The rail was a metal pipe 18 inches off the floor of the bridge and that was it.

Mother had many memories of this place near Frisco, Oklahoma. She remembered her girlfriend that lived across the field. She always wanted to go play with her, but Granddad didn't let her go over to their place. This was a mystery at the time, but looking back she knows why he wouldn't let her go.

At a revival meeting in 1922, they were invaded by the KKK fully dressed in white sheets and hoods. The crowd sat quietly as the KKK terrorized the group. That is, all but little Vona playing on the straw covered floor looking up under the hood of Mr. Thompson her friend's father. She was pulling on Granddad's hand and pointing as she said, "There's Mr. Thompson. Hey, there's Mr. Thompson."

"Quiet," said Granddad as he pulled Vona to him. He was hoping that no one heard her as she exposed the identity of the KKK member.

While living in the house across the Boggy from Frisco, Oklahoma, in about 1923, Everett left home to seek his fortune. Aim had made him finish eighth grade which was necessary in those days. When Everett returned, he found the house boarded up and the family had moved to Western Oklahoma.

Granddad and his brother Joseph Preston 'Plez' decided to go to Western Oklahoma to grow cotton. Plez had come home from WW1 and married Verna Vada McLaughlin on Dec. 6, 1919, in Onley, Oklahoma. Plez had been away serving in WWI when the sisters, Emma and Tinna died. Mother remembered the trip to Madill, Oklahoma, to show Plez and his new wife the graves of his sisters.

Bettie Patton lived in Madill and hadn't seen her son Plez for a long time.

In 1924 Plez and Verna joined Aim in a farming adventure. They lived with Aim and kids Lee and Vona and worked in the cotton fields near Martha, Oklahoma. Plez and Verna had one stillborn daughter, named Jimmie Jean Taylor, May 28, 1921. (Born and buried in Bigheart now called Barnsdall, OK), They adopted two wonderful children when they lived in Western Oklahoma near Mangum.

It was 1925 before they rented a place near Eldorado. Vona stayed with Plez and Verna while Aim and Lee went back to Frisco to move the teams and all they could to Western Oklahoma. (John A. Hart's book got lost in this move)

Remember that Everett is off seeking his fortune. While Vona is with Aunt Verna and Plez, they hear a stranger calling. That was a familiar voice to Vona so she flew out the door and down the lane to meet her brother Everett. She was so pleased to see him since she felt so alone without him as her caretaker. Her Dad and brother Lee were in Eastern Oklahoma moving their belongings to this new place.

Everett stayed and spent Christmas with Vona in this new part of the country where they were moving. That winter included some pleasant memories of ice skating on the pond and having Everett around.

Others in the family including Aunt Mollie's grown kids and their families would come to Western Oklahoma to pick cotton in the fall. Irene and husband Alvie Thomas, Pete, Lona May, and Joe Clark (Mollie's relative) were among the cotton pickers. When Mother and I visited with Joe Clark, he told about a memory from the cotton picking days. Aim's big house became the camp headquarters and the place where women cooked for the crew. Clark had only one arm as a result of a shooting accident, but he was always in charge of drawing the water from the well. Joe showed us how he would wrap the rope around his short stump and continue to pull. He said, "Aim had given the orders that the women were not responsible for the outside chores. The boys had to bring in the water."

In another story related by Joe Clark, he assured us that he could keep up with the best of them with his one arm. He told of the time he and Alvie were snapping beans in a race with Pete and Irene. Joe and Alvie snapped 709 pounds and Irene and Pete snapped only 704 pounds. Joe always found a way to keep up using one arm. That sounded like a lot of beans to me, but there was a big crew to feed.

In the summer of 1926, Mrs. Susan C. Walden Hart died. Aim came from the house and met Vona at the fence. He put his arm around her and she put her head on his shoulder and cried when he told her Grandma Hart died. She remembered her hand on Grandma Hart's shoulder as she watched Grandma Patton buried five years earlier in Frisco, Oklahoma. Uncle Joe Hart wrote a piece for the newspaper regarding his mother and Aim's grandmother:

A Sainted Mother Passes Away

Mrs. Susan C. Hart was born May 22, 1840, and died June 25, 1926, at the home of Mr. and Mrs. John Wesley Hart, near Clarita, Oklahoma. She had been very feeble for three months, and on account of old age, having arrived at the age of 86 years, one month and three days, she peacefully gave up this life, to take up her abode with those that have gone on before. She was the daughter of Mr. and Mrs. C. Walden. In the fifties, they immigrated to the sunny south and located in, what is now known as Weatherford, Parker County, Texas, which, at that time was a thinly settled country. On August 5, 1856, she was united in marriage to Mr. Joseph Hart. Being the first couple married at Weatherford, and the license, being the first issued there, the license was donated and they married in a tent, one block from the temporary court house, situated on the grassy knoll. To this union, 11 children were born, of which only one survived the mother, his name was Joseph J. Hart, who is 63 years old, he was with his mother the last six months of her life.

The family came to Oklahoma in 1889, in the territorial days and located in what is now known as Pontotoc County, and 36 years ago, Joe J Hart established a post office, which was named Hart, in honor of the Hart Family, at which place, Mr. Hart died June 13, 1898, at the age of 75 years and was buried in the Hart cemetery. Mrs. Hart obeyed the gospel at the age of 14 and lived a consistent Christian life for 72 years and died in the triumph of a living faith in Christ. Besides her son, she leaves 27 grandchildren, 16 greatgrandchildren, and 8 great-great grandchildren and many other relatives and friends, to mourn her departure. She was a true companion and a loving mother, and was loved by all, who had the pleasure of knowing her. She is gone: but not forgotten. Funeral services were conducted by Elder R. S. Baker, of Colgate, Oklahoma, and the remains were laid to rest in the Moore Cemetery, two miles south of Clarita, to await the resurrection morning. There, she will join the blood washed throng.

****

Uncle Joe had two boys and when they moved to Model, Colorado, they stopped to visit with Aim in Western Oklahoma.

Years later in the town of Model, Colorado, Vona and I talked to an old man named Charlie Shehorn that knew the Harts. He had moved to Model, Colorado, near Trinidad when he was much younger. He told a story about the silk stockings and a caper that Uncle Joe's boys were involved in. The lane that he pointed to became known as Silk Stocking Lane.

There was a great-grandson of Uncle Joe's that lived in a neighboring town. We visited with Ernie and Amy and his family and he was a tease and had a sense of humor like John A. Hart that came to Weatherford with his grandmother Mahala Hart in 1856.

****

Vona grew up and attended school in Western Oklahoma. She and her brother Lee helped their Dad by driving the car and tractor because Aim preferred not to drive. He was an expert with a team and picking cotton, but the driving he liked to leave to the youngsters. Mother did most of the tractor driving, but Aim certainly could drive.

One day the school bus got caught in a bad snow storm. The driver Jack Bybee was just an older kid about the age of Uncle Lee. The bus could not move and there were no heaters in the bus. There were benches down the middle of the bus and around the edges, so the driver told the kids to march around to keep from freezing. It was quite a while before they were rescued by Aim and another neighbor on tractors. They pulled the bus out of the drift with the tractors and got the students home safe and sound.

Granddad went to town each week to get the Sunday paper and buy supplies. Mother enjoyed reading the funnies. Aim kept up with current events and continued his interest in world events throughout his life. Granddad had read about the Panama Canal and Hoover Dam. He got to visit Hoover Dam on the way to California in 1939.

Mother was raised by her father and he catered to her. She got to go to the movies every Saturday. She realized as an adult that the movie was a good baby-sitter so her Dad could do his shopping. He was not very strict about what she bought. She could buy the pretty shoes she wanted rather than think about practical matters.

During High School, Fred Star one of Vona's teachers wrote books. She kept copies and loved to read and share them. Vona played basketball for La Homa High and traveled all over the county to compete. Girls had strong basketball teams with lots of fans and they were number one in the area when Vona played.

Vona's life was disturbed in 1932. The Great Depression and the Dust Bowl caused Aim to give up the farm because the price of cotton dropped so low that he couldn't make enough to pay the cotton pickers. President Roosevelt had a good program to stop the over production. The government paid the farmers not to plant, but it took cash money to lease the land. Only the rich could afford to pay for the lease and then apply for government subsidy. Mr. Payne took advantage of this opportunity. He was already wealthy so he leased up all the ground around Eldorado, Oklahoma, including the ground that Aim had farmed.

My Granddad and Uncle Lee had to retreat to the Kiamichi mountains for subsistent living. They had a little money and because of the extremely low prices during the Depression Granddad bought a small place back in the hills. He left Vona in Western Oklahoma to finish high school.

Granddad's big Bible shows signs of regular use. He would read to the family and he would discuss Revelations and any other subject. I never saw him attend church, but he lived his religion. He did not show hate or contempt for anyone until Mr. Payne visited in California in the 1950's. Payne acted like an old friend of the family, but Granddad had not forgotten what this man did during the Depression. He had the cash so he reaped the rewards of President Roosevelt's farm subsidy program while the real farmers had to retreat or join the CCC camps or starve.

Part II
Mahala Hart

John Hart married Mahala Niblack
and begat **Joseph P. Hart**
Robert C. Hart and others
Joseph Hart married Elizabeth Sharpe
and begat George Hart
John A. Hart
Joseph Hart later married Susan C. Walden
and begat **Mahala Elizabeth (Bettie) Hart (Taylor, Patton)**
Joseph J. Hart
Tom Hart and others
Robert Taylor married **Mahala Elizabeth (Bettie) Hart**
and begat **Amos Edgar Taylor**
Leslie Taylor
Leroy Taylor
Plez Taylor
Tinna Taylor
Emma Taylor
Maude Taylor
Kate Taylor
Amos Edgar Taylor married Timpie Leolin Southerland
and begat Everett Perry Taylor
Vera B Taylor
John Lee Taylor
James Owen Taylor
Vona LaVoyce Taylor (Wilks, Wilson)
Elbert William Wilks married **Vona LaVoyce Taylor**
and begat Imogene Wilks (Speed)
Vera Lou Wilks (Turner)
John Wesley Wilks
Mary Kay Wilks (Buford, Baker)

Weatherford, Parker County, Texas

August 1995, I visited the places that were graced with the presence of my granddad and his family. Joseph P. Hart and his new wife Susan C.Walden Hart lived in Hart, Indian Territory, Oklahoma, but they moved there from Weatherford, Texas, where Joseph's mother and extended family lived. Joseph and Susan named their first daughter Mahala Elizabeth (Bettie) after Joseph Hart's mother Mahala Elizabeth Niblack/Niblock Hart.

The older Harts came to Weatherford, Texas in 1856. Mahala made it all the way but her husband John died shortly before they reached their destination. (Mahala Elizabeth Niblack/Niblock Hart was born January 2, 1803 in Clark County, Kentucky. Her husband John was born March 31, 1794, in North Carolina.) She traveled from Indiana with her husband, children and two grandchildren in 1854. They boarded a steamboat with two dogs, horses, six children and two grandsons. Mr. John Hart, Mahala's husband, died while they camped at the mouth of Nolan River, Johnson County, near Cleburne, Texas. The Hart family was joined by Joseph, the father of John A. and George, and cousins that already lived in Texas. The arrival of Mahala and her children was at a time when Parker County, Texas, was being formed.

The county seat of Parker County was named Weatherford and laid out to be sold. On August 12, 1856, Mahala and her son Robert C. bought the spot on the square where she built and ran a hotel. The first gracious dinner party of Parker County took place in Mahala's tent shortly before she bought the hotel property. Mahala, daughter of William Niblack of Kentucky, and the children were camped at Cleviate Springs near the present day Columbia and Walnut Street in what became the town of Weatherford, Texas.

The grandsons John A. and George were sons of Joseph P. Hart and his first wife Elizabeth Sharpe Hart. The grandsons that made the trip were half-brothers to Bettie, my Granddad Taylor's mother. Their father, Joseph, was born September 21, 1823. Joseph P. lived in Madison County, Kentucky when his first son was born. John A. was two years old when his brother George was born (1852) in Dubois County, Indiana. Their mother died when George was two weeks old.

Joseph left his young sons in Indiana to live with their grandparents. John A. was about four years old when he headed westward to their new home in what later became Weatherford, Texas, with his grandmother Mahala Hart and family.

John A. Hart wrote an account of this time in his life.

We came down to Texas on steamboat. I remember when we started, that Grandfather Hart shipped his horses and two dogs on the boat. One of the dogs was a bull dog, and would not allow any person to touch him. In order to get him on the boat they circled a beef hide around him and pushed him on. I don't remember anything else until we landed in Texas, and the first thing I remember then was John Hart, a cousin of mine, coming to borrow fire. When he got to the road a big rattlesnake lay before him. The two dogs I spoke of, tackled the snake and killed it, but the snake bit the bull dog, and the dog went to Nolan river about half a mile and lay all day and night in that river. Nolan river heads in Johnson county, near Cleburne, now the county seat. Grandfather died here near the mouth of Nolan river.

I was now five years old and had begun to take notice of things that passed. We left Nolan river and moved up to Parker County. I remember on the way we camped at a place called Hams Hole, where there is a rock at the head of a flat that finally makes a ravine. At the head of the flat is a rock standing up edgeways, leaning over south, about one hundred yards long and is a fine place to camp under for shelter out of the rain or cold weather.

We camped here several days and father caught a turtle, the first I ever remember. They cooked it for dinner, and said all kinds of meat was in the turtle. This is the first thing I ever remember eating. I never saw Hams Hole any more until I was about twenty-five years old. I had pictured the rock as being a mile long, fifty feet high, and was fooled to find the rock not possessing the above mentioned dimensions.

We moved up in Parker county and there I lived for thirty years. I remember when Weatherford, county seat of Parker, was laid off in town lots. I think this was in 1856. My grandmother built the first hotel in the place. She had a well dug for water and after digging about eight feet, the digger left on Saturday evening not to return until next

29

Monday morning. Grandmother was then camped at the Cleviate springs, so I slipped off and went to the well and jumped in just for fun. I didn't think of how I would get out but soon found out that I was a prisoner in the well.

I hallooed for help but no one came. It grew dark and I was in a fix. Everybody was hunting for me. I went to sleep, after I wore myself out. A young man by the name of Norton came along looked in the well, woke me up and pulled me out. I have always had a dislike for wells ever since.

Some time after this the same John Norton that pulled me out of the well pulled me out of a hole of water and saved me from drowning. I went in swimming by myself and got too far out just as he came up and saw me.

Father married again and moved out in the country. A man by the name of Lumslin taught the school and I went to school to him. William Parsons, now living at Clarendon, Texas, was one of my school mates at the school. I will mention him hereafter. Mr. Lumslin gave me a flogging, so this was two whippings I got that I remember but I might have gotten a hundred more, but I don't remember them. At this school a young man named Emerson played preacher and took Tom Eubanks and myself in the creek to baptize us. He held us under so long we got mad and he liked to have drowned us. He baptized us until we promised to be good, so he said we were good Christians.

I never saw Tom Eubanks any more for thirty years. We met accidentally; we had camped for dinner at the same place. During our conversation with each other the subject of baptism came up and Tom related the experience he had at school. By relating the circumstances we recognized each other for the first time. While Emerson was baptizing us Parsons hallooed 'duck 'em good, souse 'em in'. After school we went home part of the way together and William Parsons and I had a fight about Emerson baptizing me. I don't remember which whipped, but I guess I got licked.

****

Joseph P. Hart, John A Hart's father, married Susan C. Walden in, Weatherford, Texas, on August 5, 1856. Susan was born in Missouri, May 22, 1840, so she was sixteen when she married a man seventeen years her senior. This was the first marriage at the temporary court house so the license was free.

While they lived in Texas, Joseph and Susan had a daughter on November 29, 1859 named Mahala Elizabeth but they called her Bettie. Soon after Bettie was born, Joseph P. Hart left to serve in the Civil War. He joined with an Illinois Volunteer group. Story has it that he came back from the war while his daughter Bettie was playing in the yard. He was so ragged, dirty and bearded that Bettie was frightened by her own father.

In the Civil War records the Stone River Campaign refers to Corporal Hart of the 38th Illinois Volunteers. He was stunned and disabled by a cannon ball. The brigade had been reduced from 7,000 to 700 and greatly discouraged.

A son, Joseph J. was born January 20, 1863, in Parker County, Texas. Uncle Joe, as he was known to my Granddad, lived to old age and spent time in Model, Colorado where I later met his great-grandson Ernie Hart.

Joseph P and Susan C Hart moved to Indian Territory to the area that later became Hart, Oklahoma. This is the area where the Southerland, Hart, and Taylor families came together.

Robert and Bettie Taylor

March 12, 1876, my great grandparents Bettie Hart married Robert Taylor in Pauls Valley, Oklahoma. Pauls Valley and Hart are near Roff, Oklahoma. Bettie and Robert lived near Bonham, Texas when three of their children were born. My Granddad Amos Edgar Taylor was born November 26, 1882, while they lived in Bonham. They moved to Arkansas where Kate was born and back to Indian Territory by 1890 where Maude, Plez, Tinna and Emma were born.

Robert's father Pleasant Taylor also lived in Bonham and he stayed in the area. He remarried after Robert's mother (called Shabby or Shavey) died. When I drove through Bonham, Texas, I looked in the phone book for Taylors and there were so many that I closed the book. I was sure many of these were descendants of Pleasant Taylor!

Robert Taylor, my granddad's father, was born March 8, 1850, in Mississippi and died February 4, 1901. When Robert died his son Amos Edgar Taylor was the oldest living at home so he worked to keep his brothers and sisters in school. Aim was eighteen, Leslie was about sixteen, Kate thirteen, Maude ten, Plez seven, Tinna five, and Emma three.

The Southerland's also lived in Hart, Indian Territory, when Annie was born (January 1894) and when Jessie was born (November 1895). The other Southerland children were born in Texas where John Henry and Sally Edna Traylor met near Cooksville, Titus County, Texas. Sally's brother Jim had descendants still living in Daingerfield and Cooksville area when Vona and I visited in 1995.

These families moved around to keep in touch with their extended families. The occasional letter and frequent moves kept families in touch. Often times it was not only relatives but also friends that made up a caravan of pioneers working together to establish new communities.

The Southerland's started out on the banks of Canada River and because of malaria and the death of one child they were persuaded to move to Hart and established a ranch just 1/2 mile west and south of the Hart cemetery. John Henry traveled a lot but he also had cows and farmed. Amos Edgar Taylor also known as Aim later became John Henry and Sally Edna Southerland's son-in-law and good friend. Aim and Timpie Leolin Southerland were married July 10, 1904.

****

Social issues of the time are discussed in the McGee-Indian Territory newspaper. Pauls Valley is very close to Hart. Notice there are no Negro pupils in the Hart School picture on page three.

MCGEE - INDIAN TERRITORY
THE CHICKASAW NEWS
VOL. 4 MCGEE I.T.(Indian Territory)
THURSDAY NOVEMBER 8, 1906 NO. 51
NEGRO IN THE SCHOOL

Cam Galt, *who returned from Pauls Valley Monday, brings the report that **Judge Dickerson** has ordered the public schools of that place open to the admission of negro pupils. He says that **H.M. Carr**, the Republican candidate for the constitutional convention, is pushing the matter. The judge ruled that equal opportunity to attend schools must be provided for the negro pupil and as no separate school had been provided the schools already in operation must be open to them. The ruling caused intense dissatisfaction in the Valley. So far, no negroes have attempted to attend the schools. According to the U.S.*

Constitution, provision ought to have been made at Pauls Valley for a separate negro school. But the white people will not stand mixed schools.

****

John Henry and Aim made a lengthy trip to the Kiamichi Mountains in Eastern Oklahoma. The purpose of the trip was to render bear grease for the care of their harness and wagon wheels. It took many weeks to kill, render the grease, cure the meat and dry the hides. They lived in the mountains in a crude camp for weeks so they were bearded and grungy when they came back to town.

Granddad's story related to this trip was about the only time he won something. There was a drawing for a rocking chair at the store. He bought a ticket which he regretted when he found out the winner had to come up on the porch and sit in the chair. With camp dirt and beard he came forward and sat in the chair embarrassed but grateful to have won the prize.

The Kiamichi mountains held a pleasant memory for Aim and when the dust bowl and the depression interrupted Granddad's farming he retreated to the mountains. My Uncle Lee and Granddad drove the Whippit car into the Kiamichi mountains. Uncle Lee wrote a detailed, repetitive, diary of driving around trying to shoot some food and camping in abandoned cabins. He chronicled crossing the river and driving where no roads blazed the trail and how cabin fever overtook them during lengthy rain storms.

Granddad bought a spot just across the river from an organized camp. There was a large home for the family that ran the camp and cabins dotted the area. Many wealthy people came to hunt and fish. My Granddad guided serious hunters, but most of the men wanted to drink and fool around up and down the river. Aim kept a pond stocked so at the end of the day they could stop at his place and buy or have their picture taken holding a long string of fish.

The Camp was there when Mother and I visited. Mother pointed to the other side of the river where Granddad's cabin had been and the bend in the river where she almost drowned.

Part III
Kiamichi Mountains

Amos Edgar Taylor married Timpie Leolin Southerland and begat:
Everett Perry Taylor
Vera B Taylor
John Lee Taylor (Uncle Lee)
James Owen Taylor
Vona LaVoyce Taylor (Wilks, Wilson)
Vera B and James Owen died before two years of age

Everett Perry Taylor married Elzina Dawson and begat:
Peggy Taylor (Borba)
Edgar Taylor
Leo Taylor
Connie Taylor (Schultz)
Barbara Taylor (Herzog)

John Lee Taylor married Jessie McCarns and begat:
Harvey Taylor
Married Fairy Rose Laird and begat:
Michael Amos Taylor
Raymond Taylor
Pat Neal Tayor
Married Mildred Langdon and begat:
Eddie Taylor

Vona LaVoyce Taylor married Elbert William Wilks and begat:
Imogene Wilks (Speed)
Vera Lou Wilks (Turner)
John Wesley Wilks
Mary Kay Wilks (Buford, Baker)

Kiamichi Mountains Including Uncle Lee's Journal Dec. 2, 1932

Vona La Voyce Taylor grew up in Western Oklahoma. She was in her junior year of high school when Aim had to give up the farm. He had weathered three years of dust and depression fall out. He was raising cotton, but he couldn't get enough money for the crop to pay the pickers.

The Dawson family lived in this area and Everett married Elzina Dawson. She didn't receive Vona very well. Elzina was jealous and possessive of Everett's time. Vona had counted on her brother as a caretaker and it was hard to give him up, but that she had to do.

Mother needed her brother after enduring surgery. Aim thought she would be better off at her brother's house so Vona was staying with Everett and Elzina. Vona knew that Elzina was possessive of Everett and had no love for her, but she was upset when she overheard Elzina complaining to Everett about 'that girl'. Vona said not a word but went back to her house swollen and hurting after having her tonsils removed, rather than stay where she was not wanted. Aim wanted her to be with her brother to watch her closely because another student not as hardy as my mother had died with appendicitis because they just thought it was a stomach ache and gave him castor oil. Even though Everett was not far away in distance, he was far removed from Vona's life.

All was not roses during High School, especially the devastating news that her Dad, brother Lee and Elzina's brother Junior Dawson were leaving to find a place for subsistent living outside of Nashoba, Oklahoma, in the Kiamichi Mountains.

Aim & Lee & Vona by the Whippet car

The morning of her father's departure, Vona was waiting on the corner to catch the school bus. She watched the Whippet car pulling a four wheel trailer go by. Her Dad was sitting straight and assuming a stoic stance as he left Vona and another period of his life behind. Vona missed the bus and returned to the old house and cried herself to sleep. Everett found Vona curled up on an old mattress on the floor. He took her 1 3/4 miles to Bartie and Buford Bryant's where she stayed.

Vona had just one more year to finish High School so she stayed behind and lived with a neighbor. She resided with Bartie and Buford Bryant until she graduated from La Homa High in June of 1934.

Once Aim, Lee, and Junior Dawson arrived in the Kiamichi mountains they wrote letters to Vona. So she knew where her Dad settled and after graduation she was able to visit by taking a bus ride out of Mangum and hiking the last few miles.

My Uncle Lee's diary gives a blow by blow account of the travels in and around the cabin that they finally bought. This was a major life change for twenty-one year old Lee but he was enjoying the adventure. In his own words, "It almost seems as if I have lived this way all my days. A person can easily drop into a new life when thinking of it would seem hard." They had been through so much from December 2, 1932, to Jan. 31, 1933, when they finally closed the deal on the funny little house. It was in the bend of Little River across from the Kaiser Fish Camp so Aim made friends and soon had work leading hunting trips and keeping fish for the city dudes.

****

Uncle Lee's Diary

Uncle Lee, Vona's brother, kept a diary of the trip and I have included his journal in this part of my story: It was recorded in pencil, faded by age and the edges were frayed during the fifty years before I transcribed it.

December 2, 1932---Thursday-----------Dad, Jr. (Dawson), and I left about 8 o'clock and lost Jr.'s clothes and a sack of flour before we got to the highway. Stayed in Altus (Oklahoma) until 11 o'clock. Made it to the Washita River 2 miles out of Wenewood and camped. June (Jr. Dawson) griped and complained and Dad told him he had wood patrol. (He would still have his clothes if he'd of tied them on good.)

Friday--------Got to Clarita about the middle of the day and ate lunch and went pecan hunting. We stayed the night with John Hart and Aunt Molly. About 480 (bunch) of us went in 2 wagons to a pie supper. Irene, Pete and Jonny (Lona May's husband) furnished the music that got better as the bottle was passed around. Pete auctioned them (the pies) *off and Lona bid 18 cents and a possum for every pie and raise bid up. ....had the ....*(The pages were written in pencil and faded and worn)

Sat.-----------Got a hound pup from Pete and left for Clayton, got there all tired out about dark. So we went to bed. Sun.----------Camped on Little River some place and killed 2 squirrels and we all went hunting and walked about 6 miles and never found anything. Dad caught a fish. Drove through the Kiamichi Mountains nearly to Arkansas. And went South about 30 miles and drove half way back and camped on Little River. Too late to go hunting but saw plenty of deer. Hung our hound pup.

Left Little River--crossed mountain to Kiamichi River again. Drove off down in the bottom and camped. Squirrel climbed the tree and got in a hole before June could get a shot off. We walked all day long to try to find out what kind of country we are in. We set some traps late this evening.

Thursday.----------Dad found a place for sale but found out they had a hog law in that county so he wasn't interested. We have stayed here a few nights waiting for Ely and Lee Baitey but we are leaving tomorrow I guess. (Ely is the father that brought his son Lee to Aim to straighten out. Remember the rope burn and the buck shot.) *Found lots of hazelnuts in the bottom not far from here. Broke camp about 9 o'clock and went to Rattan and wrote Sis a letter and went to Little River again and camped at Cobbs Crossing. Dad and June are both give out from the hard strain on their nerves from when I missed pine trees by a fraction. I was scared stiff most of the way over here too but I am beginning........................ by now..............*(a rat ate the corner of the tablet.)

Sat. 10th-------------Rained all night and got most of our bed wet. We didn't sleep much. Dad wanted a slicker for a night gown but I want an umbrella because a slicker is too cold. June and Dad worked most of the evening trying to keep the bed where it would keep dry.

Sunday 11th --------Cloudy day. June and I both shot at a squirrel but we let it get away...........hunters. (Rat ate the corner.) *Haven't seen the sun for nearly 3 days. Just got back from setting traps. June and Dad are both gone and I'm just a little lonely but I don't want anyone to accuse me of being. I don't know what time it is but I have to cook dinner. so long I was just thinking I wanted something to do. C you later. Dad and June came in with ....(Rat eaten) and cooked it for dinner.*

Monday 12th:----------Walked 418 miles got lost and found 42 times, jumped 10 deer and never fired a shot. Found out my buckshot was all 10 gauge shells. June and I jumped 10 deer in one herd. June said, "Their tails were 4 ft. long and 2 ft. wide." But I told him, "They're not more than 3" long and 1" wide. Said they........................(Worn)

Still Monday---------I filled one pocket full of buckshot. And about 1 mile from camp I filled the other full of hickory nuts and walked over a million more before I got back to camp. When we jumped the deer I found my buckshot was for a 10 gauge gun and when I got back to camp I found all my hickory nuts were rotten.

Wed.------------Cloudy all day but cleared off this evening. June and Dad both killed a squirrel ....and I tried fishing but soon got tired and quit. June set his hook in 2 inches of water. June tore his overalls in 2 places. O, yes, June's squirrel was the first he ever killed.

Thurs. 15----------We were all going hunting today but it clouded up last night and it was sleeting when we got up. I got up Built a fire and started breakfast. June got up and helped me. We got everything ready and Dad got up and ate breakfast. Then the snow began to fall we moved our fire by the cabin to keep....................................dry ....fix...............wished................Christmas, NOON It's really pretty scenes to see in a log cabin window by the fire and watch the snow drifting through the pines between here and the mountains across the creek. Snowed all evening and still snowing. Snow is about 8 inches deep.

16th-------------Followed Dad all day til after dark in 1 foot deep snow. Anyone that ever hunted with him can tell you what that means. (My Grandad could always out walk the young men that hunted with him) *We trailed a doe and ....herd for several miles until we gave out. We jumped them twice and then started home. About a mile and half from where we started back we jumped more deer and Dad shot one.................................he staggered......................jumped 6 feet up the mountain.................followed him for 3 or 4 miles straight away from camp. His feet were dragging but so were ours.*

Sat.------------Hunted all evening. Dad hit one and followed blood spots decided he may have shot her in nose. Dad was afraid his gun wouldn't kill a deer. Shaved and wrote some letters. Started to Ringo to mail. No boat on this side of river so gave them to.....................We went hunting again but ground was frozen so I made too much racket walking to find a deer. Heard one running that had jumped up in front of me. June and I were hunting together. We separated once and got lost from one another. I stopped to eat huckleberries and he got..........of me.

Tues. 20th----------Another hard days walk and no venison but it was my fault. I got another chance got a good shot and missed. I thought if I could get where there were deer with a good Winchester I could kill one but now I am not so sure. But try again is what I am going to do. I jumped and trailed them I jumped them again but never saw nothing of them the last time but there tail. June stayed at camp and swept the cabin. Put up the bedstead so we're really at home I guess because its all we got.

21st----------Dad and June went NE I went SE. They jumped 2-- June shot 2 times---they were too far away for shot guns. I never got anything but lost. I wondered around and walked about 25 miles before I found camp and I'm tired and I've got 10 risens on my neck. Dam old Ted anyway he must have gave them to me. Say but it was a queer feeling to be lost in these mountains where you can walk for miles and not see a house. I ran on to a pretty little Indian girl leading a big dog and she helped me to get straight. She said her brother and uncle went through the woods a lots and knew the way. I'm give out Heard a panther scream.......

Thursday 22----------Sometime between 10 and 2 o'clock June and I are sitting on top a mountain on a big pine log nearly give out wondering if we should get on back to camp. Everything looks wild-- the trees are dripping water, heavy fog in the air. See you tonight The weather has changed now snow, sleet, rain and fog. Dad just now said he had to go in because the weather is changing. We're having a singing tonight. We have all sung a song but I can't get the tune and haven't heard them over a hundred times. Friday Rain, rain Dam the rain. It's been raining since I can remember except the other day when it sleeted and snowed. This cabin only leaks in 4 or 5 places. Water is not but about 2 inches deep around our campfire. Everything is lovely but I can't kill a deer. But that is ok as long as the squirrels last. Again you can't hunt them without getting wet. June and I have been playing on the log rafters. He said that we were playing that we were hoot owls but I suggested---rain crows and won out.

Sat. 24th----------Christmas Eve night but I know that old Santa can't find me but this is going to be a lonely Christmas for me. Have only 17 risens on my neck and split my finger to bone trying to pick out walnut kernels. We finally got 2 squirrels for breakfast. Fried and made gravy. June and I have made a bet on what direction a fallen tree lays that we passed the other day. If he wins he gets my cane fishing poles. If I win I get his and he has to cut me 2 more straight ones. Merry Christmas Eve and oh, yea, we haven't got a chimney and my sack has holes.

Sunday 25------------Christmas but it seems like everything we celebrated by walking about 10 miles lost in the brush so thick that I could hardly walk. And I had a carbide light attached to my cap that comes down on my risen covered neck. We jumped a coon but he took down a branch (of creek) and old Queen lost him. Our light went out and we had to come in and walk a foot log in the dark. The hounds have made our deer hunt a new bedding ground. These darn risens bug me---feeling bad all the time.

Monday:12-26----------June and I went to the store today. Got a letter from Everett and Sis, all the Christmas presents that we got. I bought some scissors and am going to cut Junior and Dad's hair but I have to wait til my risens get well.

12-27------------Cut June and Dad's hair--they both satisfied with the job. Good thing because if they complain I will sure fix them next time. We killed 4 squirrel and one fish today. Some hound ran a deer close to camp but we were too late getting our guns. Got a squirrel for breakfast.

28th--------------Moved again camped on Glover Creek but it's almost a river. It runs right by our camp and the train comes along every few minutes hauling logs to the main road to be taken to Idabelle for sawing. June is playing the French harp so I will have to quit. We have lots of different homes. Had to leave my fishing poles, too long to put in trailer. This is an odd life. I am lonesome, gay, downhearted, light hearted by turns.

Thur. 29th----------Raining again. But let her come--I don't care. We got our sheets stretched again--I sure miss that cabin. I killed a squirrel last night and this morning with one shot I thought I was sitting good but shot twice and let one get away.

30th----------------Cleared up this morning and clouded up late this evening. Rained awhile and now it's clearing up again. Then load more logs on the fire. Just pitch them on the flat car. Dam the smoke I got to go to bed.

31st.---------------See you next year. Last day of the year. June nearly ran a deer over me today but I didn't have my gun. I been wanting a cinch. Well I got it today but no gun. Guess I will have to eat bacon or squirrel for New Years. From now on I'm going to carry my gun even if I'm going nowhere but..........................

Sunday 1-1-1933----------Wasted a few more shells today on a deer. Got a standing shot out about 150 to 175 yards and missed so I still have room to improve but still got hope. We have company tonight but leaving tonight. Have to eat pig and squirrel. When I start my book in 1932 I wondered when I would have a home to go to. Now I wonder if I will ever have a home. June and I with 2 more guys tried to find some deer. But we never got a good shot. They always jump up when you least expect them. My gun shoots high so maybe I'm not such a bum shot.

Jan.3, 1933-------------We took a sudden................all I can think of is Bill. Hope today we want to go North so we headed south to Right City and Valiant, Oklahoma, then to Hugo then N. to Antlers and finally camped about 5 miles NE of Fernly. Stopped out of the mountains about 2 hours. Was I glad to see them again. We are moving on tomorrow I don't know where and I don't much care.

Wed.---------------Still wondering around. We've been everywhere and part of the way back. We went to Mush and Pine Valley but turned around and came back where we're headed none of us know. I want to go S. of Clayton down the Kiamichi River and look the country over. Tell you tomorrow where we go.

Thur.--------------Promised to tell you where we went today but I don't know. We are camped way back in the mountains west of Dunbar, but I still can't write to Sis. Bet she is raising cane. I have a headache so I better go to bed.

Fri. 1-6-----------Dad knows that his gun won't shoot buckshot. He slipped up on turkeys and shot and never even scared them. Then he took #6 quail shot and shot another but both flew off. We are going down there about daylight. We moved about 2 miles but we are going to stay here a while. We have a lot of pets here deer, panther, bobcats, wolves, turkey and wild horses, skunks, and squirrels. We can't locate a P.O. closer than 8 miles--you have to go about 40 miles in a car. It rained and got the creek up so we didn't get to go after the turkeys. We have some neighbors--a bunch of guys are trapping wild horses near here. My risens are getting worse.

Sun.-------------Cleared off--going to get some Pole Cats tonight but they sure do stink. I hate to sleep with Dad and June--they both smell so much like one. I will be glad when we get their trapping all settled so I can go to hunting deer again. I have filed my sights down on my gun. Dad caught him 3 good fish and I baited a trap with one of them. June and I set traps and hunted pole cat dens. We have been in some of the worst places I have ever saw--rocks, cliffs, with caves all through them--12 or 15 ft. high.

Jan 10, 1933------------June and I had 4 box traps. Dad caught him another fish. June showed me about how to jump the creek. He made it but over balanced and had to wade down 10 steps to regain his balance. Then started to throw a stick at me for laughing a little.

Wed. Jan.------------Caught a flying squirrel and brought it in to share. June had never saw one. Climbed a tree today to stop a squirrel in its hole and went to camp after the ax. Dad and June went back with me to cut the tree down but the squirrel got by my sticks I put in the hole so all our work was for naught. IN MARGIN LEE WROTE It almost seems as if I have lived this way all my days. A person can easily drop into a new life when thinking of it would seem hard.

Thur. 12------------All's quiet on the Western front. I'm lost anywhere I go here except one place on a high rock cliff across the creek. The sun comes up in the south and goes down the north. When I cross the creek and climb that cliff it turns about 1/4 of turn and I can't tell who is right me or the sun, but I'm never wrong.

Friday 13th----------Dad and June killed 6 squirrel and saw a bunch of turkey flying into the creek bottom. They went down to try to roost but something must have disturbed them because they crossed the creek. June and I washed our heads and shaved and bathed today. What do you think of that?

Sat. 14.--------------June and I killed 5 squirrels in a short while. Say it is fun shooting these cat squirrels when they are this thick. You get in a bunch and scatter in every direction and you can't tell which to shoot first. Some of the trees are so high you can hardly kill squirrels with a 22 or a shot gun. We are going to try to write to Sis pretty soon.

Sun. Jan. 15,1933------------Fixed our load so we can leave tomorrow if it don't rain. Don't know where we are going but think we are going to Antlers, Oklahoma to find where there are some places to locate. Say but I hate to leave here on account of the squirrels being so thick I had heard of squirrels hiding up every tree at these bottoms. I saw this this a way. Dad saw one of these bulls that have big ears and hump back I don't know if there are more here. He came back to camp and said he was leaving. He said, "When animals like that run wild and Jack Asses and camels mix they should be left to the wild country."

Jan. 16th.--------------Say but this has been a pleasant day we broke camp and started out this morning early. Worked hard all day and we are camped on the creek bank about 100 yards from our cabin with our car in the creek and it looks like rain and we feel like hell. Our car won't crank and we are having to bail out so we can push it. June wondered what we would do if there was no sawmill pit here and Dad said, "Hell we wouldn't be over here."

17th------------Dad and June walked to Kosona and borrowed a battery-- They couldn't find one for sale. They could carry everything in their tow on their back. Stayed at camp by myself and couldn't go hunting for fear the hogs would root our bed up. I got supper ready just as they came in about dark.

18th-----------We left and got to Antlers and put up for the night and wrote a couple of letters home and ate supper at a table with a tablecloth. 1st time in about 7 weeks and went to the show after supper. Saw "Prosperity" played by Marie Dressler and Polly Moroni or Morrow. IN THE MARGIN This day reminded me of the day Carl Dawson, Ted and I went to Nashoba last winter.(Carl kept a diary of that trip)

Thur. 19th------------Left Antlers and are camped on Little River and intend to wait for an answer from Everett and Vona. We are camped just below where Carl, Ted and I camped our 1st night on Little River.

Fri. 20th.-------------Had to stay in camp because I put on some beans and I had to watch them. Dad and June went a squirrel hunting and never found but 1 they could get.

21st Jan.------------Rained all day nearly. We had company all evening. Two brothers one from Tuskahoma and the other lives near where we are camped. Come down and talked all evening with us. As we dodged from the fire to the tent as the showers came and went.

22nd.---------------We moved about 2 miles today to get to a drier place to camp. Dad and June located the place while they went squirrel hunting. They came on back and we moved up when we crossed at the spot where they picked Dad wanted to know if it looked like home, I looked around and saw some pine trees, a post oak, and big log to build our fire by and said, "YES". IN MARGIN: Oh!Yea! I baited out the hooks and trout line to take them up and move. Got a chance at a deer and missed. I am not even pretty good.

Tues. 24------------Wash day. June and I washed today at a queer washing. We got to some rocks out in the creek and went to work. Had only one advantage. We had an unlimited water supply. June is singing so loud I can't think. Wed. 25th.-----------Say but I'm getting handy, washed yesterday and today sewed and patched. Washed and shaved now what do you think of that. I have been reading and June setting up with me has whittled out a pile of pine knot shavings about a foot high for fire that he has to build in the morning.

26th------------Went to Nashoba yesterday and couldn't hardly carry off the mail but I was getting ready for it because I hadn't heard a word since Christmas. (Mr. Butler's Store and the same Mr. Butler saw Aim Taylor in Ada, OK on Granddad's trip in 1957. He recognized and came out to greet Mr. Taylor)

27th-----------Wrote 5 letters believe it or not and went down the river to deal for a little place but the guy down there pulled out so much whiskey we forgot to trade. We mailed them letters late this evening. Fool Sis when she gets it because she won't be expecting an answer so soon.

28th----------Cut June's hair and washed mine. Cooked beans while Dad and June went a deer hunting. But they can't find any. They don't know where to look. But it don't do me no good to find one, I can't hit them.

Sunday Jan 29,1933------------Went back to see the old man we are on a deal with. He had about 60 gallons of whiskey. Said it would probably last him all winter since he only drank about 1 quart per day except Sunday and Holidays---then he drank 1/2 gallon.

30th------------Killed me 2 squirrels a while ago so we could have it for breakfast. Hung it on a tent stake while we went to bait some fish hooks and when we got back old Queen had ate all of it but the tail.

31st.----------Caught 8 fish last night---made a good mess for dinner. We have already caught 3 little yellow catfish tonight. And have another one on the throw line. And we bought us a home today. It sure is a funny looking home but a good one. signed: LEE

<u>Last entry of Lee's journal:</u> And we bought us a home today. It sure is a funny looking home but a good one. signed LEE

****

Vona in Western Oklahoma

The Depression and Dust Bowl hardships took my Granddad away from Western Oklahoma. Vona was left behind to finish High School. Bartie and Buford Bryant provided a good home for Vona. She had Aunt Verna and Uncle Plez close by and Vona loved to go to their house to play with Mary Jo. Her brother Everett and wife Elzina lived in the neighborhood, but they were not much comfort to her. She finished her Junior year in 1933 participating in all the school activities. Vona was good at basketball.

The field trip with the school would take on great significance later in life. The school visited Granite Mountain in Granite, Oklahoma. One of the attractions was a reformatory for young men in Oklahoma who worked in the granite quarry. Little did she know that her future husband, my father, was an inmate there. The reformatory didn't get him straightened out since he had a family involved in 'bootlegging'. He was caught later crossing a state line in a borrowed car with 'white lightning' and did more time in Texas and in a federal penitentiary in Atlanta, Georgia. That's another story and comes to Vona's attention three years later after the next chance meeting in 1936.

Vona graduated from La Homa High in 1934. Graduation night many friends, including Aunt Verna and Uncle Plez, and her brother Everett and sister-in-law Elzina attended. Vona was thrilled to see Everett, but later she found out that she needed to thank Mr. Dawson for the honor. Mr. Dawson was a commanding force, but only 4'5" tall. He had spoken to his daughter Elzina and son-in-law Everett saying, "Vona is graduating next week. She has done it without family behind her and if you two don't show up at her graduation I will never speak to either of you again."

Graduating during the Depression left very few opportunities for a young lady. Vona moved to Mangum, Oklahoma, to live on the cotton farm with Aunt Verna and Uncle Plez. The most she could do was baby sit for Mary Jo and Jim, separate the cream, and help around the house. When a job in town came up she moved to a room in town and soon started working in a bakery. Vona was a trusted employee and had the keys to lock up the store. One day she forgot to lock the door and couldn't remember how she got home.

Vona found herself losing memory for brief periods of time. She realized that these were not normal occurrences, so she went to the hospital. Good fortune was with her since one of the doctors on staff recognized her condition and was skilled in the surgery. Being raised in Oklahoma goiters were common. There was not enough iodine in the diet so the thyroid gland did not work properly. Vona's goiter was growing inward leaving no outward signs. To prevent payment responsibility being thrown onto anyone else she told them she had no family.

While Vona was being operated on, Lee, her brother, came into town and found her. He got to the hospital in time to view the operation through a glass. Bloody, bloody--he didn't watch much, but he did get the word to Aunt Verna and Uncle Plez that Vona was in the hospital. It had been over a year since Vona had seen Lee--just a coincidence that he came to Mangum that day. Lee would leave and drop in from time to time with stories of riding the rails and visiting California.

Vona healed but wore the scar at the base of her neck until she died March 20, 2002. She went back to odd jobs and spending summers at the cabin in the Kiamichi Mountains with her Dad. The summer of 1935 she caught a bus out of Mangum which was a hub of transportation.

Aim, her Dad, didn't know she was coming so getting to the cabin was an adventure. The bus went as far as Antlers, Oklahoma, but that's over thirty miles from Noshoba and the cabin was about seven more miles into the woods. Cardboard suitcase in hand, Vona started walking knowing full well it would be dark before she could get where she was going.

'Expect to find a way and I guess you will,' must have been her thought. Walking along she noticed a truck come by with a hitchhiker on the tailgate.

'Boy, I wish I had gotten a ride,' crossed her mind but didn't slow her pace. Later she found out that the hitchhiker was responsible for the driver coming back to pick her up. She spent the night at their place. The room was small, but they made a pallet under the table so she could sleep.

The next day Vona made it to Noshoba and stopped at Mr. Butler's store. She knew that no one would be there to greet her since they didn't know she was coming. Lucky again, it was Saturday and a dance was happening that night. Mr. Butler assured Vona, "Aim will be in town for the dance." Being the new young lady in town, Vona ended up dancing every dance and sure enough her Dad was there to guide her home that night. Quite a welcome for a nineteen year old.

The direct route that Mother and I traveled the summer of 1995 seemed short, but Mother remembered an entirely different route which took her to the other side of the river and to Aim's cabin. Vona remembered dancing with Skeet Fuller in particular-- good dancer. This made the chance meeting with Skeet's wife, son and granddaughter a delight. The brief visit with Charlie Fuller, Skeet's son, was enlightening. Charlie had visited California many times. He ran around with Harvey Taylor, Uncle Lee's boy. As he told about the place where they went to steal gas from a big tank mother said, "Yes, that was my place."

Skeet's wife remembered trips to California to pick peaches for Lee and Mother. She recalled the years that she brought her kids to pick prunes also. She had fond memories of 'fruit tramping' in California. Vona took her memory back to the dances and fun of the summer of 1935 before she married Skeet.

Mother remembered a time when she cleaned Aim's cabin on one of her visits. There was a very important old black rag that Aim used to clean his grill and a huge spider web that hung over his chair. Vona got the rag burned and the web down, but she found how important they were when her Dad got back. The web was used as a mosquito net when he was reading in the evening. A rag could be replaced but that web he couldn't redo.

Another time Vona was out walking with her Dad. He just sat and watched for awhile. He noticed the direction of the honeybees. Knowing that bees make a beeline home when they gather enough pollen let him know where to go rob a honeycomb. That was important knowledge when you wanted honey for the company that was visiting.

While we were talking about the cabin and the bend in the river by the Kaiser Fish Camp, Skeet's granddaughter recognized the spot on the river.

"Yes, the Marlin Fish Camp is deserted, but still there. That's my swimming hole," she said. "Would you like me to drive you down there?"

"Sure," Mother and I blurted out.

The dirt road took us to the back side of what used to be called the Kaiser Fish Camp. I thought it was a fish hatchery but instead it was a camp with cabins for rich people to rent. This is the place my Granddad had told me about. In 1933, Granddad rented boats to the fishermen and provided guide experience. Granddad told me when I was little about the rich fishermen and hunters that would come by his cabin. He kept a pond in back stocked with fish so the city slickers could drink and clomp around the mountains up and down stream and return to have their pictures taken with a string of his fish. He would even sell them a string of fish to take home. Granddad served as a guide if a serious hunter wanted to pay him. My Granddad knew the woods and the river because he had hunted there many years before with his father-in-law John Henry Southerland. Aim lived through the Great Depression in the Kiamichi mountains that he knew and loved.

Vona worked the summer of 1935 for the wife of the man that ran the Kaiser Fish Camp. She took care of the kids and helped around the house. The main house was still there--remodeled-- but recognizable.

**Vona standing on the bank of Little River
showing where she almost drowned**

Knowing that the old man Kaiser drowned in the river right at that spot reinforced the memory of mother's adventure with her brother Lee. The river was much higher in her memory and Lee's job was to take Vona to work in the boat. One day Lee goaded Vona into swimming across. The Fish Camp and Granddad's cabin were on a bend in Little River just below the junction of Black Fork and Little River. It was way to swift for Vona to swim and she almost drowned in the process, but she was standing on the bank of Little River telling the story August 2, 1995.

Part IV
Decisions That Led to Texas

At nineteen life decisions must be made. Vona decided she didn't want to stay in the mountains with Aim or on the farm with Aunt Verna and Uncle Plez. She went back to the town of Mangum to get work waiting tables.

Timpie, Vona's mother, had a number of sisters and Mary Tom tried to stay in touch with her niece, Vona. Mary Tom knew how to reach Vona on July 14, 1936. She got the news to Vona that her Grandmother Sally Edna (Traylor) Southerland had died in Roff which is the closest town to Hart, Oklahoma. Vona's cousin Robbie (Aunt Lenore's daughter) had a picture of Vona taken the day of the funeral.

Sally Edna Southerland was buried at the Memorial Park Cemetery in Ada, Oklahoma. Vona was in the company of relatives that she didn't see very often. She met Sally's brother Uncle Jim Traylor from the Cooksville, Texas area. Grandpa Southerland, Uncle Jim, Mary Tom and Mr. Cox (Mary Tom's husband) took Vona in a Model A to the Kiamichi Mountains to see Aim. During this ride Vona became reacquainted with her mother's relatives. She learned that two aunts were now married to husbands that worked for the railroad and lived near Tucson, Arizona.

On the way back from the brief visit with Aim Taylor, Mr. Cox said, "Your Dad is a smart man. Why is he throwing his life away staying in the hills?"

Vona didn't have an answer, but those who knew my Granddad realized this was a retreat to wait out hard times. Granddad never voted again after the Depression. He always said, "My vote is too powerful so I don't vote. After the stock market crash in 1929 and the Great Depression, I couldn't find anyone else that would admit they voted for Herbert Hoover."

Vona went back to Mangum and soon heard of a two week job in Elk City, Oklahoma. She went to work in a restaurant on Main Street and was surprised the last day of her job when a familiar customer stopped in.

"No wonder I haven't seen you in Mangum. What are you doing here?" asked the customer.

"If you had stopped by one day later, you wouldn't have seen me this time," quipped Vona.

"What do you mean?"

"I'm going to Tucson, Arizona, tomorrow."

"How?" asked the customer.

"If you're going my way, I guess," was the well thought out answer.

The man realized that Vona had no purpose in going to Tucson, certainly no job and she didn't even know the married names of her aunts.

"You need to try Sulphur Springs, Texas. I think you can get work there and if you don't you can go to Tucson from Texas just as easy as you can from here," offered the customer.

The next day Vona left Elk City, Oklahoma, heading for Sulphur Springs, Texas. The cotton seed salesman had a stop over in Oklahoma City so Vona waited in the car and then on to Texas. This kind fellow paid two weeks rent on a room at the old Jefferson Hotel and made the contact so Vona had work during lunch rush for two hours a day.

Vona met Mr. Caruthers who was the Banker's son. He was looking for a cook in a restaurant owned by Sid Pogue(Pronounced with a long 'o' sound) in the booming town of Sulphur Bluff, Texas. He asked if she could cook and Vona said, "Sure." Never cooking in a restaurant before didn't deter the precocious Vona, she expected to find a way.

Sulphur Bluff was a thriving oil town with a healthy business district. It had sidewalks and many homes on the side streets. Oil wells surrounded the town. The oil activity soon dried up when the wells quit producing. It was the fall of 1936, and the beginning of a severely cold, wet winter.

The restaurant also needed a manager to stop employee's from stealing from the 'til', and I wonder if they needed a little 'moonshine'. Sid brought in a new business associate. Vona was busy washing table legs since mud was everywhere. The new associate came in with coat collar pulled up around his neck and hat pulled down over his face. Sid introduced employees to the new associate.

"This is Vona, our new girl."

"What did you call her?" asked Elbert Wilks.

"Vona"

"I can't say that. I'll call her Jimmie." So that was Vona's new name. People that met her after that day knew her only as Jimmie. Vona LaVoyce Taylor became Jimmie and was soon to become a Wilks.

My father renamed my mother Jimmie that cold, wet, winter day. In the street in front of the restaurant the oil rigs were moving out of town leaving ruts so deep you would fall in chest high if you tried to cross the street. Sheets of ice were hanging from the power lines in December of 1936. Deliveries were impossible. The town came to a screeching halt.

Christmas Day was memorable since Jimmie and Elbert spent it together snowed in the restaurant. The menu was put together from current stock, no supplies had been able to get into town for days.

It was January 1937 when a Standard Oil representative that frequented the restaurant took Jimmie and Elbert to Dallas, Texas, to get married. Their courtship had been short, but they knew that this was a soul mate connection and they were ready to get married. On the way Elbert finally confessed to the friend that he had a wife somewhere. He had married an older lady named Jewel when he was a teenager. According to the 1930 census Elbert was nineteen and lived in Louisiana with his wife Jewel. "Elbert, I'm not the one you need to tell. You better tell Jimmie before we get to Dallas." With this complication, they didn't actually get married. But they did consider this a marriage and it lasted until Elbert's death June 17, 1954.

The trip to Dallas was a well deserved vacation. The oil man that had business in Dallas was off doing his thing while Elbert and Jimmie stayed at the hotel where they met one of the other patrons.

The fellow had a party going with Jimmie and Elbert and a room full of people when he got a phone call. He looked a little pale as he hung up the phone. He turned to the group and said, "The jigs up. They've got my brothers and they're on the way over here." The group was surprised when the fellow opened a closet door and showed them the shelves full of counterfeit bills. "Take all you want. It's not doing me any good."

Jimmie and Elbert had never seen so much money in one spot. They didn't take any of the money but it sure broke up the party. Naturally, they didn't forget the incident. In 1974 Jimmie, now married to Fred Wilson, was working with Sam Blankenship and renting from him in Hughson CA. Sam and Jimmie were surprised to realize that they were both in Dallas and aware of the counterfeit caper. Sam Blankenship was an observer on the other end of the event and was aware of the brothers being arrested at the train station just before they got out of town.

Jimmie and Elbert had some good times. The dance hall on the outskirts of Sulphur Bluff was built for and frequented by the oil workers. The juke box had been moved in by Elbert and Jimmie. Just one crash getting it moved had scarred a place down low on the back side.

The job in Sulphur Bluff ended and the town was 'drying up' when the oil boom died. Suspiciously, one night the dance hall burned to the ground. The insurance paid for the loss. Jimmie and Elbert rode from here to there doing short jobs and making contacts with family and friends to try to find work.

One night they stopped in Tyler, Texas, at a jiving joint to dance awhile, the room was crowded and the music great. The juke box never stopped playing. Elbert walked over to the juke box and soon motioned for Jimmie to come look. He pointed to the familiar scar on the lower back side. Now they knew for sure the fire was no accident. Much of life seems like one coincident after another.

From 1937 to 1939 Jimmie and Elbert stayed with family, went out on small jobs, and worked hard to survive. Mother had driven tractor in Western Oklahoma so when Daddy got a job with a tractor she helped him to know how to start it and what the levers would do. She was belittled and harassed by her mother-in-law Myrtle, but Elbert appreciated the help. He was good with a team of horses, but had never driven a tractor.

Some of the Davis clan was in business. Uncle Bob was making the moonshine, Granddaddy Wilks and Lillian had a store serving as an outlet. Now all they had to do was get the alcohol from the source to the store. That is where the milk haulers helped. Uncle Ben Davis and Aunt Mary had the milk route for years. On the Wednesday night run, Aunt Mary loved the stop at Granddaddy Wilks' store because she got to raid the candy counter and get a Coca Cola with the kids Don and Dorothy while the grownups unloaded the moonshine.

Mother told me of one job that they did out of New Orleans. The contact point was the first real 'speak easy' she had seen. That was the only job Daddy did for his famous cellmate Al Capone. In order to keep the stills going they had to have plenty of sugar. This job was on a banana boat that went to Jamaica to get sugar. Sounds silly for sugar to be illegal, but the intended use of the sugar was illegal.

My Dad gave up his illegal deals and became a family man. Imogene was born November 9, 1937, in Golden, Oklahoma, one of the places where Elbert's clan lived and had a productive still. Also it was near Valiant, Oklahoma, where my great-grandfather Van Davis is buried and Broken Bow where Uncle Sonny, my grandmother Myrtle and Leonard's boy was born.

Imogene's birth was early and extremely difficult. Mother started labor pains and Daddy had to ride into town and get a doctor. The doctor came out and he actually stimulated the labor. Mother had been having pains for days and during the final stages the doctor used forceps on Imogene's head and pulled her out. Mother was exhausted, after the baby was born the midwives put Imogene in bed with her. When Mother woke up, her arm was on Imogene's face and her baby was almost dead. The doctor gave orders for mother not to get up.

In a short time, Aim found out where Imogene had been born. He bought a bassinet and went to see his new granddaughter. As soon as he got there he started moving Mother. He told her to start exercising or she might never get up. By the next day he had Vona on her feet. Mother never forgot this lesson. Mother referred to this every time she was in charge of a recovery process. Even on her death bed in March of 2002 she tried to get up and exercise.

Earlier when Jimmie first took Elbert to meet her Dad, he recognized the region. Just over the hill was the hot spot of activity that he knew about as a child. Lots of whiskey stills were in operation in the 1920's and 30's. According to Uncle Lee's journal the fellow that Aim bought the cabin from had sixty gallons of moonshine for his own consumption.

Elbert Wilks, my Dad, had little chance to grow up without trouble. His mother Myrtle Marie Davis Wilks Anderson was not a good role model. She was born on October 31st and displayed many witch characteristics. Her father Van Davis was running from the law most of the time. L.E. Shelton, called Sis, was Myrtle and Willie Davis' mother, but she died when Myrtle was very small. Sis washed her hair during her time of the month and that sealed her fate. You may have heard the old warning to women not to wash their hair during their period. The family truly believed that is how my great-grandmother died. After her death, Van left Alabama with Myrtle and Willie riding horseback. Hannah, Van's sister cried as she watched those two cute little kids riding off with their mean, irresponsible father.

Van married Unis (Eunice) in Texas and had Jeff, Ben, Jerome, and twins Roy and Floy in between his stays in Alabama, Texas, Oklahoma and jail. My grandmother Myrtle and my great-uncle Willie were the older half brother and sister of these kids. They were raised as a clan and all helped in the illegal ventures and maintained the clan qualities through my father's life. When they married the spouse became part of the clan or they were ridiculed. My Mother was criticized and tormented with gossip and untruths.

When I visited with Arthur (pronounced Auther) and Jewell Davis in 1978, Arthur told me some stories only after I let him know that I knew what was going on during those days. My Dad's mother and dad divorced when he was about fourteen years old. Myrtle had been a somewhat respectable mother and wife up until the divorce when she returned to the clan and married Leonard Anderson. Elbert and his brother Thurman spent most of their time with Myrtle and the clan.

Arthur shared an incident related to a time when Elbert came to his place. He had ridden a freight train and was just a boy on the run.

Willie Davis' girlfriend Suzie Moyer got Elbert to cash a bad $50 check and split the money with her. He got it done, but got caught and taken to the police station. Myrtle, his mother, was brought in and she begged to talk to her son that was in trouble,

"Maybe I can talk some sense into his head." She was allowed to talk to Elbert in private and about that time a train whistle blew. Myrtle said, "Son, you think you can make that jump and catch that train out of town." It was a two story building, but Elbert made it. When she saw him catch the train, she ran out of the room waving her hands and crying, "Lordy, mercy, I don't know what I am going to dooo with that boy; he has jumped out the window and run off."

Elbert was tired, hungry, and scared when he arrived at Arthur and Jewell's house in Sulphur Springs, Texas. This was not Myrtle's first performance. Another time Myrtle had helped her brother Willie and others steal a load of hay near Peerless, Texas, where she lived with John Wesley Wilks. This time she pretended to be pregnant on the witness stand and became hysterical to divert the questioning. I guess she was a good actress.

Arthur drove me around Hopkins County where my family had lived. Peerless was a community riddled with outlaws. That is where my father was born and spent much of his young life. People in Sulphur Springs where Arthur lived had commented on how good a person Elbert was and questioned how he could come from such a place.

Elbert was influenced by the clan, married in his teens and worked the Louisiana side of the business. He tried from time to time to do other jobs. One was working on 'oil derricks'. He stayed with Arthur and Jewell and bought a pair of white pants which Jewell remembered vividly having to wash, starch and iron. Elbert didn't do too well working for others, he always had a business idea. One such idea landed him in Texas State Prison.

Elbert borrowed a car and went to Valiant, Oklahoma, to get a load of whiskey. He planned to make enough money to pay for the use of the car and get a start. He came across some other boys that were hanging loose and up to no good, they joined him and had a different idea. According to Arthur, they loaded the moonshine and drove away without paying. The owner of the 'still' fired his gun at the car and they were on the run. They were caught and convicted. The prison time that Elbert did in Texas was traumatic. He watched a young inmate get trampled to death by the guards. The new inmate just asked for a drink of water and the guards told him, "Sure," and motioned to the water wagon and dipper. On the way back to the chain gang the guards on horses with whips ran back and forth over the young inmate until he died. My Dad couldn't have been much older than twenty-one himself.

My Granddaddy Wilks lost most of his money paying for lawyers and court costs to get my Dad out of Texas State Penitentiary. He was successful, but the car had crossed state line so the federal charges sent him to Atlanta, Georgia, to the Federal Penitentiary. The conditions were better. Instead of a chain gang, the inmates had jobs. Elbert worked in the laundry, he could iron and sew very well, but when I was little I never saw him do either. By this time it was 1934 and Al Capone was in the cell next to him. Capone was assigned to laundry so Daddy made friends with the infamous criminal. He watched the guards come in and tear pictures off his cell wall. Capone was a family man and he wanted the pictures of his family gracing the cell walls. Each time he put them up the guards would destroy them. August 19, 1934, Al Capone was one of the first inmates to be transferred to 'The Rock' as Alcatraz is called. My Dad stayed in Atlanta until he was released in 1935 to his Grandparents Joe and Mollie Evans Wilks Lovell. Daddy spent a year working on his grandparent's farm using horses to work the land.

John Wesley Wilks was not exactly innocent when it came to moonshine. He had a 'whiskey still' in Peerless, Texas. When the two workers were cooking it off in their smokehouse, they were raided. John Wesley, my grandfather, got a two year sentence. Pa Lovell was able to get a pardon before he went to prison, but the two Negro workers did time.

John Wesley married Lillian Barron after the divorce from Myrtle. They had two kids Don and Dorothy and ran a store in Hagensport, Texas, just fourteen miles from Mt. Vernon. The kids could eat all the candy they wanted so they were very plump and Lillian was huge. The story goes a customer asked if she was raised on ELEPHANTS MILK. She was so mad she threw cans at the customer until he got out the door.

I visited Dorothy Nell Wilks Harville Vawter at her house in Gridley, California on June 3, 2006. Before Grandaddy Wilks and family moved to the Haggensport store they had something brewing out back. Dorothy remembered, even though she was only four (1933), her job was to wipe the foot prints with a leafy branch. When they walked through the woods to the STILL she would wipe the trail to a natural state. She also remembered the call from neighbors. If the Revenuers rounded the corner on the main road, the relay of the message started. REVENUERS COMING, REVENUERS COMING, REVENUERS COMING. They were never able to sneak up on the cookers and this 'still' was never found. Later the Hagensport store was receiving shipment of bootleg booze from Uncle Bob Davis' STILL by way of the Milk Truck.

John Wesley died in 1946 from a heart attack and is buried in the Begota Cemetery. Lillian came to California with her new husband Perry (Pep) Jones, stepson Zack, and about 200 pounds lighter. She lived into her 90's and is buried in the Biggs-Gridley Memorial Cemetery.

A visit with Arthur and Jewell in 1978 added a lot of knowledge of the family since Arthur (pronounced Auther) was a self appointed historian. In 1952 my Dad made a trip to Texas and asked Arthur to take him to Alabama to the old home places. Arthur worked for the road department and didn't think he could take the time off so they didn't go. Elbert died June 17, 1954, so Arthur didn't get to show him. He was delighted to take me to Alabama because he felt he was paying a debt to my Dad.

**Arthur Davis
and Elbert Wilks
in 1935**

**Arthur Davis
and
Elbert Wilks
in 1952**

In 1978 when Arthur and Jewell took me to Alabama we stayed with Helen and E.J. Howard in Athens, Alabama. Helen was the youngest child of a Davis girl in a cousin line. She had completed an extensive family history of all the relatives of my great-grandfather Van Davis and she let me know that Van and Bob were the black sheep of the family. At church they would sing loud and off key. They were always in trouble and both of them had gone to Texas and married sisters, Unis and Aunt Bert. Part V details the 1978 visit to Alabama and will take you back to the beginnings of Elbert William Wilks' side of the family. In August 1995, Mother and I stopped at 515 Mulberry Street in Sulphur Springs, Texas. This had been the home of Elbert's double cousin Arthur Davis and his wife Jewell. Elbert had come to stay with Arthur many times in his turbulent childhood. Since Arthur's death Sam Evans another cousin bought the house. Our surprise visit was announced by me.

I asked, "Are you Sam Evans?"

"Yes," was the questioning reply. I introduced myself Vera Turner and made the mistake of saying my mother Vona Wilson is with me. Sam Evans remained confused as to who we were. I continued telling him my father was Elbert Wilks and that his wife Vona and I wanted to see him. Soon he realized who we were and welcomed JIMMIE and I to his home.

Part V
Davis/Wilks/Evans family lines

Squire James B Davis
Son: Larkin Davis begat next to the youngest:
Van Buren Davis married L. E. Shelton (Sis) and begat:
Myrtle Marie Davis
Willie Davis
married Unis Davis and begat:
Jeff Davis
Roy and Floy Davis
Ben Davis
Myrtle Marie Davis married **John Wesley Wilks** and begat:
Elbert William Wilks (my father)
Thurman Joseph Wilks
married Leonard Anderson and begat:
Louis Weldon Anderson and a twin boy that died.
John Wesley married Lillian Barren after the divorce & begat:
Don Wesley Wilks
Dorothy Nell Wilks (Harville, Vawter)

....

William Wilks married Louisa Jane Vick and begat: many
children & John Wesley my Great granddad who died in his
twenties.
John Wesley Wilks senior married **Mollie Evans** and begat:
1. **John Wesley Wilks jr.** married **Myrtle Marie Davis**
and begat: **Elbert William Wilks (My Father)**
2. Rosa Wilks married Oscar Davis and begat:
Arthur Davis double cousin and good friend to Elbert Wilks

Limestone County, Alabama

In the 1800's the **Davis/Wilks/Evans** families came together in Limestone County, Alabama area near Good Springs. Summer of 1978 Arthur Davis led the way to Good Springs. He said, "Take Market Street out of town (Athens, Alabama). Then the road is called Buck Island Rd. or Hiway 99. There is a big hill about halfway to Good Springs," Arthur continued, "this is where they had to put the brake on the wagon to keep the wagon from running over the horses. Oh, and over to the right is the Jackson place."

Arthur, Jewell and I went north to the community of Oak Grove in Good Springs. Inez Sinyard owned the property around the pre-civil war house. She lived in a mobile home and the old house was open so we went in and looked at the stairs leading to the short upstairs.

Arthur at the spring in front of the Pre Civil War home of
James B Davis

Pre Civil War home of Squire Jim Davis

There was a fireplace in each end. No kitchen because the cooking was done outside. Arthur said, "Squire Jim lived here with his slaves upstairs. Later, they were just his workers after the freeing of the slaves."

Squire James Brown Davis was born in Georgia May 5, 1813, to Larkin Davis and his mother. November 5, 1835, Squire Jim married Elizabeth Covington with family ties to France. Elizabeth had children from 1838 until 1864. Elizabeth was born in Limestone County October 25, 1818.

Squire Jim gave the property for the Good Springs church to be built. Grandpa Evans was the preacher at the time and the whole community built the church. Two hand hewn pews were still in the back of the church the day we attended in 1978.

Arthur pointed out the spring in the front yard of the pre-civil war house where they kept the milk cool and drew water for the house. Arthur Davis drew a cup of water from the spring at the home of Van's grandparents Squire Jim and Elizabeth Covington Davis. Van's father James Larkin Davis was the second born child of Squire Jim and

Elizabeth Covington (born December 2, 1839). James Larkin was named for his paternal grandfather and was called Lark. Lark was killed by a runaway horse and buggy in 1881, a year before my Grandmother Myrtle Marie Davis was born. Lark was married to Almeda F. Jackson and is buried in Good Springs Cemetery in Limestone County, Alabama. The 1880 census in Limestone County Alabama shows James Larkin Davis 40 years old and Almeda Jackson Davis 38 years old. Some of the children were already married but the ones in the house in descending order of age: Thomas C. eighteen. William F. fifteen, Elizabeth Jane twelve, Mary A. ten, Mack J. seven, Vanburen H. four, John R. one (this is Uncle Bob). Hannah and Virginia Lee (Ginny) were not born yet. Squire Jim and Elizabeth Covington Davis raised Hannah and Ginny and Helen Howard's father James Burgess Davis who was three years old in the 1880 census.

The cemetery across from the church is filled with Evans and Wilks graves. The preacher of the church at the time it was built was Grandpa Evans, father of Mary Lou (Mollie) Evans Wilks Lovell.

Mollie was married to John Wesley Wilks when he died of a heart attack at about age twenty-six. He was chasing cows across the pasture when he dropped dead. Arthur and Jewell Davis and I attended church the day we visited this area. When the small, friendly congregation found that we were descendants of Rev. Evans, Mr. Thurman Sinyard said, "Oh, then we must be relatives. I call him Uncle John Evans." Another lady was so glad to see us and pointed across to the hillside and said, "Oh, John and Mollie lived right over there. My mother knew them and we still call it John and Mollie's place."

The Oak Grove Cemetery is just across from the lane that leads to Squire James Brown Davis' plantation home. Just up the way is the church built on the property of Squire Jim Davis and the Methodist Preacher was Rev. John Wesley Evans. Rev. J. W. Evans also worked at the grist mill just south of the church and he had an active hand in building the church and pews. When I was there in 1978, Rev. John Wesley Evans' picture was still hanging on the wall.

The church had been modernized and most pews were store bought, but the last two pews were of the hand hewn wood worked by the original builders of the church. Patsy Wims, daughter of Sam Evans, has the Rev. J.W. Evan's picture and the two hand hewn pews.

After church, Arthur and Jewell Davis and I walked the Oak Grove Cemetery. I found my great-grandfather John Wesley Wilks that died so young. He was just twenty-six or so and died of a heart attack while chasing cows in the pasture. He was married to Mollie L. Evans, Rev. Evans' daughter. They had two children Rosa Ann Wilks, Arthur Davis' mother, and John Wesley Wilks, Elbert's father, my grandfather. Rosa and John each married a Davis so this made Arthur and Elbert double cousins. We turned left out of the cemetery and made the next left to drive by the grist mill where Rev. Evans worked and further on we made another left to the old home place of Mollie and John Wesley Wilks where they lived at the time of his death.

Their home was close to the Evans Cemetery at the top of the ridge. This is the ridge that one older member of the congregation pointed to when she found that we were descendants of Mollie and John. Her Mother had personally known them at the time my grandfather was born and his dad died the same year (1890).

Mollie and her father Rev. J.W. Evans moved to Texas around 1900 and she had not heard from them until we showed up for church in 1978.

Mollie's mother was also buried in the Oak Grove cemetery. The stone read Malisa A. Evans, but she is listed in various documents as Melissa A. Wickham, born 9-15-1845 and died 12-1-1888. The tale told about Malisa A. Wickham Evans is that during the Civil War she screamed so loud that the Yankees didn't take her horse.

Rev. John Wesley Evans and Malisa A. had nine children. All the children that lived to be adults are buried in Texas. The whole bunch made it to Texas.

Joe died at about age 21.

Mollie L., my great-grandmother, was born in 1867 and died 1944. She is buried in Mt. Sterling Cemetery in Hopkins County, Texas, by her second husband Joe Lovell.

James Owen(Jimmie) was born 19-7-1870 (this must be a misprint or read 19 day of July 1870) and died 1-8-1920. He married Mintier Cundiff and had no children. He is buried in Peerless Cemetery, Texas.

Sallie, born 1873 and died 1945, married James Billingsly and had eight children named: Etta, Ezra, Ellie, Effie, Rachel, John, Lilla, Minnie. She is buried in the Emblem Cemetery. This is where Rev. John Wesley Evans is buried and in 1999 there was a Civil War Ceremony to honor J.W. Evans a Confederate. There is a sword in the family that John Wesley Evans brought home from the war. He was a part of the Confederate Army and they captured a Yankee wagon train and pulled out the sword before they burned the supply wagons.

In 1876 Johnny was born and later married Agnes Davis. Their children are Bessie, Rominor, Jeff Davis, Bascom, Marvin, Sam. (The son Sam is the man that Mother and I surprised in 1995 and he didn't recognize who we were because I called Mother Vona instead of Jimmie as he knew her.) Sam's father Johnny is buried in the Emblem Cemetery.

Robert Samuel died at less than a year old and is buried in Evans Cemetery at Good Springs, Alabama. (Born 6-24-1879 Died 3-9-1880)

Martha Elizabeth (Mattie) and her twin Lidia Ann were born 6-27-1881. Lidia Ann died just before she turned four and is buried in Evans Cemetery at Good Springs, Alabama. Mattie married George Bullington and they had no children. Mattie was buried in the Emblem Cemetery at her death 3-28-1949. When Elbert took his family to Texas in 1948, Aunt Mattie and Uncle George were on the list of people to see.

Bayless Wheeler Evans, born 1-26-1887 and died 2-21-1978, married Ida Maude Edmonson. Their children are Gladine and John William. He is buried at the City Cemetery Sulphur Springs,Texas. Bayless' dad, Rev. John Wesley Evans, served as a Confederate in the Civil War under General Joseph Wheeler. After the war he named his last born son, Bayless Wheeler Evans, the 'Wheeler' being a namesake for General Wheeler. Later, after the war, by chance they ran into General Wheeler and Grandpa John Wesley Evans told the General that he had named his last born son after him. General Wheeler took a quarter out of his pocket and gave it to Uncle Bayless, who was a boy at that time.

On September 4, 1861, General Wheeler was appointed Colonel of the 19th Alabama Infantry with which he fought at Shiloh. He had a busy career then moved to Wheeler Alabama in 1868. He was elected for a first term in Congress, in 1881, and thereafter served eight terms in all and is buried in Arlington Cemetery.

Rev. John Wesley Evans and Sam McConnell agreed the survivor of the two would host the others funeral. So when Rev. Evans died 8-20-1919 in Texas, Sam McConnell held a memorial service at Oak Grove in Alabama and a large crowd attended. The picture of Grandpa Evans 75 birthday was taken just a little over a year before he died. The little boy with the hat is Elbert and his cousin Arthur is beside him with a white shirt.

Grandpa Evans' 75th birthday gathering taken 1917

Young Arthur Davis and Elbert Wilks
from group picture

The original Evans couple that came to Alabama from North Carolina started this line of Evans descendants. John Evans, born 3-22-1817 and died 4-17-1863, married Mary W. Carroll. Mary W. was born, 12-18-1817, and died on 5-12-1896. Both are buried in the Evans Cemetery near Athens, Alabama, in Good Springs. John was the first person to be buried there.

Long ago the trip from North Carolina was a tough one. A son, Owen, died of measles coming to Alabama. He was only fourteen at the time of his death. Daniel C. (born 1837) and Aaron (born 1839) died while in the service during the Civil War. Rev. John Wesley Evans was one of seven remaining children. Rev. J. W. Evans lived in Good Springs, Alabama, and worked at the grist mill. Van Davis, Squire James B. Davis' grandson, was at the mill one day when the law came in looking for him. Van took his knife out and cut his shoes off so he could out run them. He did out run them even though they were on horseback. Van and his brother Bob were wild and both were good at making 'moonshine'. Limestone county was still a dry county when I was there in 1978.

Mollie Evans married John Wesley Wilks. The Wilkes' came from Pulaski, Giles County, Tennessee. The name had an 'e' in it back then but William or his wife Louisa Jane dropped the 'e' from the spelling of our name. I don't know if Pulaski is a town or region, but it is near the border of Alabama.

John Wesley Wilks died very young and his mother Louisa Jane Vick Wilks Brackeen was living in the area. She remarried William C. Brackeen after her husband William A. Wilkes died in Tennessee. They later moved to Hopkins County Texas. Louisa Jane is buried by her last husband in the Emblem Cemetery in Texas.

One of John Wesley's brothers was Burl Wilks. Burl was Hubert Wilks and Florence Wilks Brown's father, and they also lived in Sulphur Springs, Texas. Granny (Louisa Jane Vick Wilks Brackeen) as she was known lived with Florence Brown. She has no marker on her grave. Arthur knew where it had been and it was about ten paces from Rev. Evans in the Emblem Cemetery. Arthur thought she died about 1916. During clean up at the cemetery, the grave marker rocks got moved and hers was nowhere around. Her Wilks husband was killed by a run away horse in Tennessee. Arthur Davis didn't know him but he did know Granny Wilks. Granny had cancer of the nose and probably used snuff. Granny Wilks was born Louisa Jane Vick in December 1842 in Giles County, Tennessee. She married William A. Wilkes in Tennessee. My father was named Elbert William after this Grandfather.

William and Louisa had their family while living in Giles County, Tennessee.

Mary L. Wilks was born about 1861 and died before 1895. She married William Andrew Coffman December 7, 1889, in Giles County, Tennessee, son of James Franklin Coffman and Lindy Frances James.

My great-grandfather **John Wesley Wilks** was born in 1863 and he married Mary Lou (Mollie Evans). The birth date that I have is July 15, 1862 and death date February 17, 1890. The birth date doesn't fit since his brother was born 8-10-of the same year.

Wilson Fayette Wilks was born August 10, 1862 and died Feb. 20, 1948 in Wichita Falls, Wichita County, Texas. He married Ophelia Lea Brackeen.

Martha E. Wilks was born September 1866 in Tennessee and married William H. Faust December 7, 1889 in Giles County, Tennessee.

William Burrell Wilks was born Dec. 16, 1869 and died Feb. 15, 1936 in Hopkins County, Texas. He married Rebecca Brackeen July 18,1891, a sister to Ophelia Lea that married Wilson.

Zoda Wilks was born September 1875 and married Thomas McCutcheon about 1895. He was born Dec. 1874 in Tennessee.

Oscar (Bud) Wilks was born March 20, 1876 and died March 24, 1957 in Quemado, Maverick County, Texas. He married Anna Lizzie Hatton October 10, 1895, in Sulphur Springs, Hopkins County, Texas, daughter of George Washington Hatton and Martha Bartlett. She was born April 7, 1881 in Marshall County, Alabama, and died Feb. 26, 1965 in Clovis, Curry County, New Mexico. Doris Moore is the granddaughter of Oscar (Bud) and Anna Lizzie Wilks. Doris is the keeper of the web site. Thank you for the lineage.

In 2002 on the 4th of July, the Peerless community had a reunion picnic at the cemetery. I was there and talked with Patsy Evans Wims and George Wims. Patsy is the daughter of Sam Evans. Sam drove his own car and was his jovial self. Sam took my sister Imogene and I to see the place where our Grandparents were married. It was a place on a little county road number 4798 and he said that Rev. J.W. Evans had ridden a horse out to the spot to marry John Wesley Jr. and Myrtle Marie Davis. My Dad Elbert William Wilks was their first born (born. 8-27-1911 and died 6-17-1954). Thurman Joseph Wilks was their second son.

Patsy had a genealogy line off the roots web site that gave me names and places of birth and death of the Wilks family back to England. One marriage was to a lady from Wales. They arrived in New Kent County, Virginia in the 1600's and moved to Lunenburg County, Virginia. They moved through Tennessee and on to Giles County, Tennessee just before my branch of the family moved to Good Springs, Alabama.

My sister Mary Kay Wilks Buford Baker sent more information from another website. Looks to be the same names and places that our Wilks line came from.

Mollie Evans Wilks Lovell lived outside of Peerless, Texas, with her second husband Joe Lovell. Ma Lovell was important to my Dad when he was a young man. When he was let out of prison, he was released to Joe and Mollie Lovell. Elbert helped with the harvest and spent a required year with the couple. He was near Sulphur Springs, Texas, where Arthur and Jewell Davis lived. This was an unsettling time readjusting to the outside. Elbert did not go to church with the family on a regular basis. He had empathy for Ma Lovell who would sit with her shriveled, arthritic hands on the radio in hopes of being healed. This was the reason he didn't like organized religion.

Elbert soon went to work in Sulphur Bluff, Texas, in a little restaurant owned by Sid Pogue. This is the spot where he met Vona LaVoyce Taylor, soon to become Jimmie Wilks. Many from the Good Springs area ended up in Texas.

Part VI
The Trek to California

Lots of preparation and struggles went into the decision to go to California. Early one morning, Ben and Mary Davis driving their milk route took Elbert to Greenville, Texas, to catch the freight. This started the search for a place for Elbert to take his family where he could make a living.

Elbert rode to California on the freight train and stayed in Hobo camps along the way. He told the story of being thrown in jail in Arizona. The law was trying to get the vagrants to buy tickets and keep them from riding the freight trains. Daddy sat in jail that night and met an experienced freight rider. To get out of jail all they had to say was, "Yes, we will buy a ticket."

So Elbert and the fellow went to the train station and bought tickets. That took all of Elbert's money so he wasn't too happy. They turned away from the ticket booth and Elbert was lamenting the fact that they had to buy a ticket. The fellow hobo assured him it was no problem. He just put his ticket in his pocket and away they went along the track to hop the next freight out of town. When they got to California near Winters they hopped off the freight and went straight to the ticket office to cash in the ticket they bought in Arizona. My Dad bought a new pair of shoes with the money and worked a season in California.

The meeting place during the depression when the Okies were tramping around California trying to make a dollar was the Post Office so that is where Elbert met the boys from home. He met up with Mother's brother Lee Taylor, Shorty, Carl and Junior Dawson, Dick Cole, and others from his home territory. Mother and Imogene stayed with Granddad Taylor in Eastern Oklahoma while Daddy looked for a place to settle and worked so he would have enough money to make the move. Earlier, Granddad had made a trip to California on the freight train but he failed to make contact with Lee and Shorty.

The story Granddad told about his ride in California was when he almost froze to death. He had caught the freight out of Oroville and

76

rode through the Feather River Canyon. It was so cold he almost froze and then the tunnels were scary because he had to lay low and eat the smoke from the smoke stack. He was glad to get back to Oklahoma.

Granddad Taylor decided to return to California with Elbert, Jimmie, and Imogene. Aim had already sold the cabin on the river because he suffered with Malaria too often. He had a hunting dog he had to get rid of and a hog that was ready to be butchered. A neighbor that was mean to his dogs wanted Aim's hunting dog and was willing to pay for him. My Granddad said, "NO," to the fellow and gave the dog to another neighbor that was good to his animals. He thought he had the hog sold until the day they were to leave.

Elbert returned from California and bought a 1936 Ford on credit. He made the first payment and then they left for California. Later they did send money back for the car.

My Dad had seen all the 'Grapes of Wrath' type vehicles and the desperate lines of people in the dirty government camps. On the road to California he always stayed outside the camps because he did not want his family in a dirty Government Camp. He didn't want anything hanging from the vehicle so they had all of their belongings including camping and cooking gear inside the car. The four inch safety pin that they used to pin the tent closed was in Mother's box of treasures that we found when she died at age eighty-five. Carefully tucked away she also had the tiny gun from Imogene's cowgirl boots on a black shoelace.

Granddad had the hog sold and when they went to town to get the money for it the guy backed out hoping to get the pig for nothing. That was not to be. Granddad bought a butcher knife and they drove to the river bank and butchered the hog. They had to build a big fire to scald and scrape the hair off. The fat had to be rendered because that is how they preserved the meat. They layered the grease and pork until the keg was filled. This was a time consuming task so Mother and Imogene were sleeping in the car.

Near midnight they were awakened to see a complete lunar eclipse. It was November, 1939 and that event is all that Mother had to mark the date.

When the task was complete they left Oklahoma with just one keg on the bumper. The pork kept them from starving like the characters in Grapes of Wrath and others along the road. Imogene had a song she would sing on the travels. 'Down the road, and Down the road, and Down the road, and Down the road, and Over the Hill and Cross the bridge, and stop 'n eat.' All they had to do was stop and fix the HOG that was on the bumper.

November 9, 1939, Imogene turned two years old and she attracted looks and people to talk to as she walked down the street or down the rows in a cotton field. Mother remembered Christmas of 1939. They went to the city of Phoenix and walked the downtown streets just window shopping. Imogene in her new pair of cowgirl boots with the little pistol in the side pocket attracted the attention of many.

Imogene in her new cowgirl boots

My Life enters this story.

The trip to California was a real Grapes of Wrath story. Except for the keg of pork strapped to the bumper of their 1936 Ford, my folks didn't have belongings hanging for the world to see. My father was a proud man and he had a destination. He had talked to Mr. Hughes and he had a job if he could get to Gridley, California. Daddy, Granddad, and Mother worked along the way, but they made it to Gridley, California, before I was born.

The Wilks family had been camping along side the road under the trees, but had to give up the shade when the swarms of gnats started biting. They moved nearer the dump in Palo Verde, Arizona. The dump included many treasures. One useful item they used as a grate to improve the cooking pit.

When Mother and I visited the spot by the trees, Mother pointed out the power lines. The linemen were installing the wires near the Wilks' campsite. One man stopped and talked to my Granddad one day and told him about the Government Camp with running water. Granddad thanked him for the information and kept walking.

Mother's brother Lee Taylor was in California already traveling with buddies. Uncle Lee Taylor and Daddy had used the post offices and general delivery to stay in contact. My Dad had sent a map and directions to Uncle Lee who was still in California.

Lee knew his Dad and Sis were on their way to California and he was trying to get to them in Palo Verde, Arizona. In town, with map in hand, he was very puzzled. There was nothing in the direction that my Dad had shown on the map. Lee talked to a man at the post office who worked for the power company.

Lee was describing the folks that he was looking for and the lineman asked, "Is there an old Englishman that smokes a pipe with them?"

Lee answered, "Yes, and a little blond headed two year old girl."

The lineman replied, "They are camped on the other side of town and I told them about the Government Camp, but they just stayed by themselves."

Lee realized then that Bert was turned around when he made the map and following the map in reverse took Lee right to the Wilks'

Campsite. The contact with Uncle Lee gave them an update on where friends were staying near Calipatria, California, waiting for the pea picking to start.

It was great having Lee join them in their makeshift home. At dinner, when Imogene the petite, blond, two year old said, "Give me some HOG," Uncle Lee was surprised. He told his sister to teach her another way to ask for food.

Living in these conditions made it hard for Mother when she heard Daddy turn down the job on the dairy farm in Buckeye, Arizona. He had just turned down a house to live in and all the milk and eggs the family could use. That was the nearest my Mother ever came to leaving my Dad, but they did make up and got back on track because that is the time of my conception.

From Palo Verde they went to Calipatria, California. That's where friends of theirs had been waiting for a job. The friends were on more than one list to go to the pea fields. The next day after Mama and Daddy, Granddad Taylor, and Imogene arrived in Calipatria, their friends Junior Dawson and George Langdon got called to two fields so Daddy and Granddad went out to one of the pea picking jobs. They worked quite awhile in this spot because Mother had lots of stories to tell.

Actually, Mother and Daddy drove back to Yuma, Arizona, and got married April 8, 1940. Remember the story about the trip to Dallas to get married in 1936. It never happened back then so they decided to try again. I don't believe Daddy ever got a divorce from Jewel but he was clever and he just misspelled his name on the license so it couldn't be traced to him. He listed his address as Calipatria, California and Mother listed Buckeye, Arizona as her address. I don't think he had anything to worry about because there were no computers then. Mother and I got a corrected copy of the marriage record in 1995 and I also got a copy of the one typed on the old typewriter with the name misspelled.

On another driving trip they took Granddad up to see Hoover Dam. Granddad had kept up with the building of the dam in his Sunday papers. He always read it from front to back. They were on the hub of the rural electric project that lighted the country. It would be well after my brother John was born in 1942 before the Wilks house was lighted.

The Salton Sea is just north of Calipatria and close by there are bubbling hot spots. Some ladies even washed clothes in the hot water. It looked dangerous and risky so Mother didn't use them. As they neared Indio, California, on their travels, my Dad stood in a welfare line to get a mattress for my Mother. She must have been getting big with me on the way. The intake person kept asking him what aid he had received and he kept telling them none. They insulted him by calling him a liar. It truly was the first welfare that he had received and if Mother didn't need the mattress he would not have been in that line.

Mother emphasized that they never stayed in Government Camps along the way. She pointed out the place where they camped under a Joshua tree near Indio. There were lots of Joshua trees out of Indio, but she thought she found the one. The trip with Mother in 1995 was full of reminiscences.

Arrival in Gridley, California

The Wilks family arrived in Gridley, California, May, 1940. My Dad had helped Mr. Hughes with a team of horses during his 'Hobo' train riding days. He talked with him and was put in touch with the Steadman Brothers that owned the Ord Ranch. Our first home was a ladder barn on the banks of the Feather River. The ladder barn was on the edge of Steadman's peach orchard surrounded by rich river bottom soil and just a quick walk to the Feather River. Remember Granddad had made his way on the banks of Little River just below the junction of Black River during most of the depression near Nashoba, Oklahoma, in the Kiamichi Mountains.

The family ate well with Granddad's fishing and according to Imogene's story they had plenty of Pheasant also. He would always tell Imogene he shot a cottontail and then say, "Let's go bury the feathers."

The ladder barn is where we lived when I was born August 18, 1940. Mother had so much trouble with Imogene's birth that she went to Oroville to the hospital to have me. When she got home and found out that Daddy and Granddad had almost let Imogene drown in the rushing Feather River, she vowed to not leave them in charge again. I came home to a Libby lug box for my bassinet. Mother had left all the valuables along with Imogene's bassinet in Texas with John Wesley and Lillian Wilks (her in-laws). All the valuables and pictures burned, but Imogene's bassinet was saved because our cousin Kenneth Earl was using it.

In the ladder barn the studs were exposed because it wasn't finished and had no insulation. They had no electricity and had to draw the water from an outside well and haul it inside. But this was a big improvement from camping beside the road.

The Steadmans had a little house on about five acres that they wanted to sell. During the depression it was hard to sell anything. In fact, the banks owned most homes. They offered the house to each of the workers and each turned it down until they got to the last hired and Daddy had a chance to buy it. Granddad Taylor helped with the $20 down and the $5 a month payment. When they moved to the house on the five acres, winter was closing in on them so there was not a lot of work. The ladders were returned to the ladder barn where we had been living.

My Dad had some pigs that he was raising on halves and he had a garbage hauling route for the restaurants in Gridley. My Dad had plenty of garbage to feed the pigs and at the end of the season half of the pigs were his. Mother took care of the chickens and planted a garden in the spring.

Elbert Wilks was a talker and made friends easily so soon my Dad had peach orchards leased and he paid a share of the crop for rent because we had no up front money. He had made friends with June and Kay Yokatobe before they were hauled off to the internment camps for the Japanese. They were taken away about time for their peaches to be harvested. Daddy had their peaches picked and sold. The Yokatobe's were grateful when they returned after the war and their peach crop was spared.

Every spring Mother and Granddad planted a big garden so they had a produce stand to sell the vegetables and eggs. One of their best volume customers was Fred Stanley Wilson. He was buying vegetables for the Hotel in Live Oak where his mother fed people from all over. Fred was in the trucking business in those early years and later he became my stepfather.

Mrs. Weems, the neighbor lady that lived down the canal bank, became a dear friend. She visited us often after her first visit. She saw the lanterns lit a couple of nights in a row because she had sleepless nights and was just walking late in the night. Mother had been nursing a sick family. They had pneumonia and Mother was glad to see Florence Weems when she came walking down the canal bank just checking on her new neighbors.

I was little and Mrs. Weems played with me and visited with Mother. She had combed my hair one day and Granddad commented on my pretty hairdo. He asked who combed my hair so pretty and I answered with my first word, "Weemie". That is how Florence Weems got her new name and she was called Weemie even after she married Mr. Paul and until she died years later.

Weemie had the distinction of baking the first birthday cake that my Mother ever remembered. Mother's birthday was April 13th and was often close to Easter. The year was 1941 and Weemie baked a round two layer cake with coconut sprinkled on the frosting. In the middle of the cake she made a coconut nest and jelly beans were the eggs. I don't know about candles, but it was definitely Mother's first birthday cake. Birthday cake is one of those things that her Dad just didn't do when he was raising Vona.

The house was close to the big canal and one day there was a rattlesnake in the yard. The dog saved Imogene from taking the bite, but he died in the process. I was just learning to walk so I stumbled a lot and my Dad blamed himself for not having a better place for his girls.

This is the house we lived in when my brother John Wesley was born. Remember, my mother vowed she would not leave Daddy and Granddad in charge so she stayed home to have John. She was way overdue and Weemie was checking on her each day. They had a signal system set up so Weemie would know if Mother needed help. In the day time she was to hang a white sheet on the clothes line and at night she had to put the lantern in the window. John was so slow in coming that Dr. Freundenthal was called. He couldn't administer ether because he was working by lantern light. He couldn't regulate ether properly in those conditions so Mother had to give birth to a big boy with nothing for pain. John was born on March 28, 1942. Granddad Taylor had Imogene busy outside in the pasture looking for the new baby. She remembered the tall star thistles and the tiring search. She was irritated when she got inside and Mother had found the baby.

My folks worked hard because they had a chance. They worked from 'can' to 'can't' and they were always looking for another opportunity. The depression had made it impossible for them to make much legal money. Buying the little place gave them a way to turn the ground into a money crop. When W.W.II came along the opportunities opened up even more. During my growing up years we didn't have much money, but never were we told that we were poor. My parents instilled the feeling that there is always a way. If you want something you just make a plan and you will be able to get it. You never had to wonder **IF** you could do something. The decision to proceed with a plan was did you really want it or would it be good for you and certainly not hurt anyone else.

My son wrote the 'About the Author' section which helped me realize how I have internalized the idea that anything is possible. He related the story of his mother challenging the clerk at the credit union with the statement. "I am not asking **IF** the loan can be made I just want to know **HOW** you are going to do it."

PHOTO ALBUM

The following pictures were taken in the yard of the first home my family bought. We still had the 1936 Ford that the family drove to California. My older sister Imogene and I are on the front steps of the little house by the big canal.

Notice the velvet dresses and the store bought dolls.

Imogene and Vera by the 1936 Ford that the family drove to California

The little girl with the bucket in the chicken pen is Vera.

My brother John is the little boy just outside the pen
full of young pullets.

Daddy and Imogene and me at the first place the family bought in
California. Notice the hand pump to draw water and there
was no electricity in the house.

You can see from the pretty dresses that Weemie and mother made for us and the store bought dolls that the Wilks family is doing better now. This has to be about 1943. I know we were poor because when mother was in Oklahoma someone gave her material to make a dress for Imogene and she didn't have enough money to buy the thread to put it together.

Imogene actually started to school from this little house. She had to walk down the canal bank a short ways to get to Little Ernie Steadman's bus stop at the Ord Ranch. Mr. Weems made his morning walk just in time to walk with her to the bus stop.

Lots of activity one morning aroused the attention of Little Ernie. Near the bus stop a team of men were assembling to search the area and drag the canal for the elder Mr. Steadman. Little Ernie's grandfather was missing. Imogene knew about the tragic event and Big Ernie warned mother that Little Ernie didn't know and he was worried that Imogene would tell him. Mother told Imogene not to tell because Little Ernie didn't know. She was barely six years old, but she kept the secret all day. Little Ernie was speculating about all the people going fishing that morning. Imogene never said a word. They did find Mr. Steadman in the canal. He wasn't the first because the older Mr. Bettencourt from across Larkin Road had drown in the same canal a few years before.

Uncle Lee and his new wife, Fairy Rose, lived in the house by the slough just across from Weemie's place. They had running water and electricity. Because Mother now had three little kids to take care of and Imogene walking the canal bank to get to the bus stop they decided to trade houses. I remember the house we moved to because the bedroom ceiling was so low Imogene and I could touch it when we jumped on the bed.

I have a pleasant memory of helping with the dishes. I had a stool and felt like I was a big shot to help wash dishes. This is where we lived when Imogene attended McKinley school in Gridley. Her teacher Miss Whittier was young and enthusiastic and Mr. Joseph McGie was the principal and also drove the bus. Imogene was just six years old, but she remembered what a kind man Mr. McGie was and also how well he dressed. She was impressed with her bus driver.

One day at school she had a little friend who wanted to go to her house after school. Imogene was delighted, so when Mr. McGie stopped both girls got off the bus. Mother was surprised when the extra child arrived at the house but with no phone, no car and no note she just took care of the girl and as it neared bedtime the police came to the house looking for the girl. Luckily, Mr. McGie remembered an extra getting off at the Wilks' bus stop because her parents knew nothing of the arrangement. I suppose this is why a note is required for everything now.

Crops were good at this house too. Granddad grew tobacco plants that were higher than his head. Somewhere in the scheme of things we sold the little house to Leonard and Gladys Bryan who ran the East Gridley Market and Uncle Lee Taylor bought twelve acres and a house on Higgins Ave. in East Gridley.

Daddy and Uncle Lee also traded vehicles. So for many years, Lee and Fairy drove the 1936 Ford that we brought to California and Daddy got a 1934 pickup. He had to have the pickup to haul scraps from the restaurants in Gridley for his pigs. W.W.II made it difficult to get tires and impossible to get them for cars. Our whole family could ride in the pickup. Daddy drove and I sat on Mother's lap and Imogene straddled the gear shift with John standing behind her. It was a tight squeeze because the 1934 pickup cab is very narrow.

Pepper was another item that you couldn't buy during the war. Granddaddy Wilks and Lillian came from Texas to California to work in the shipyards in Richmond. They were able to get their hands on a can of pepper for Mother and she said that it was the only contraband she took, but she was glad to get it. Because of the shortage of pepper she also told me that the restaurants in order to conserve switched pepper to the shaker with small holes in the cap. Salt was now put in the shaker with bigger holes. Now they just do it because that's the way it's done. The reason was to conserve pepper so now I have to unscrew the lid to get enough pepper. Mother taught all of us to like generous quantities of pepper.

My Grandmother Myrtle and Leonard Anderson came to California about this time. They and their son Louis Weldon Anderson (Sonny boy) visited when we lived in the little red house by the slough. I don't remember much, but Imogene remembers the day that Sonny tricked her into sticking her finger in the electric socket. It was an old style round open socket. Sonny would stick his finger in part way to show her that it wouldn't hurt. So she finally stuck her finger in all the way and got a hard shock. She yelled loud enough that mother came running to help her.

Mother had one studio picture made of the three of us
Imogene age 6, Vera Lou age 3, John Wesley age 1 1/2

Mother described the difficult process of getting us ready for the picture. The yard was dirty and she would get one ready and then the other would be dirty. She was exhausted when she got us to the studio and then we were so timid and inquisitive that none of us would smile. Daddy knew Mr. Robe (pronounced Robbie), the man that took the picture, so it was one of the perks of Daddy's talking.

Because Granddad Taylor lived with us and baby sat, Mother and Daddy could get out a lot. They would ride around and Daddy made contacts for each of his business deals. They still liked to dance and in Marysville they participated in a street dance contest one night. The movies on Friday night was a big deal and became a family affair when we got big enough. On the weekends our house was always full of relatives.

Friends, aunts, uncles, grandparents, and cousins visited often. Mother always had a pot of beans on the stove. Sometimes she would kill a chicken and have chicken and dumplings. She would feed about fifteen people every weekend. As kids we loved it because we always had someone to play with. As different relatives came to California they were strangers to me because I had been born after the family arrived in California. My Dad's family lived in close proximity and the gatherings were clannish. The adults sat around and talked by the hour. The cousins became close and played by the hour as the adults went over stories from old.

It was in the first few weeks of second grade that Imogene was diagnosed with Rheumatic Fever. The treatment was complete bed rest. Dr. Freundenthal had been killed in a car wreck so the Wilks family was now seeing Dr. Frank I. O'Neill M.D. in Oroville. We took frequent trips to Oroville to monitor Imogene's Rheumatic Fever and Mother had to keep a daily temperature chart. Naturally, I wanted my temperature taken too, so it wasn't long before they realized I had Rheumatic Fever also. Imogene and I spent seven months in bed with no activity. While we were in bed I turned four and Imogene turned seven.

Our family bought a twenty acre place with a big old house on it. When they moved, Imogene and I stayed with Uncle Lee and Aunt

Fairy. We weren't allowed to get out of bed so we had to sit on the side of a crib to eat lunch. After the move was complete, they carried each of us to our new bedroom. It was much bigger and now we couldn't touch the ceiling.

Months later we got to see the rest of the house. It was a big, rambling, old ranch house. The piano, dining table and wood cook stove were left in the house. The closet to our bedroom had a back door that connected to the dining room. When we got well, this was used as a race track for chasing cousins around and around. There was also a low window from our room to the porch where Granddad slept. It was possible to run through his room but he put a stop to that.

My Uncle Don and Aunt Dorothy Nell were living in Richmond with Granddaddy Wilks and Lillian. They were young and wild. That is where Don got in trouble with his friend Lester so Daddy had to go to Bakersfield to get him out of jail. He had married Frances early on so they lived in a cabin on our property and used the kitchen and bathroom in our house. When Frances threatened to break a plate over Don's head if it were hers, Mother told her to go ahead, she didn't care about the plate. Soon Frances was gone and my Aunt Billie (Frosine Deonacia Ballas) came in the picture. Imogene and I were over the Rheumatic Fever and able to enjoy the weekend visits.

Daddy made lots of improvements to the house. Mother and Dad wallpapered the living room and dining room which had twelve foot high ceilings. Dad had the house jacked up and put a foundation under it. He also poured red circular concrete steps at the front and back doors. I remember the new electric stove and the big hot water heater that Daddy installed. The counter tops were really wooden draining boards.

There was only one real bedroom and Imogene and I got it. The long front porch was divided into a bedroom for Granddad and one for John on the other end. The back porch was enclosed so Mother and Dad had a bedroom on one end and the bathroom was on the other end with a free standing bath tub with claw feet. On the remaining back porch Daddy built a corner wood box with his half-brother Don's help.

The well was old and Daddy had it re-cased to protect it from contamination. He reinforced the barn and poured concrete to make it clean enough to sell milk. He had milk cows and an electric milking machine. He still used his milking stool that he strapped on with a single pole sticking out. I thought it looked goofy and seemed like he had a tail. It worked good because he could sit as he moved the milking machine from cow to cow. The milk was strained and put in milk cans. The 1934 pickup was used for years to haul the milk cans to the end of the driveway. My brother and I got to ride on the headlights as Daddy drove.

Daddy had reworked the chicken coups so that the manure could be scooped from the outside. This went directly to the garden area for fertilizer. Mother canned and fed us from the garden. It was my job to gather the eggs. I usually got to the house with the eggs, but I remember the day that I tried the swinging motion that I had used with the feed and water. I'm sure this is something my cousin Louis Wayne taught me. (Centrifugal force will keep the water in as you swing it round and round.) The entire bucket of eggs was broken with this great experiment. Luckily, Mother saw this as a learning experience so I didn't get in trouble. Mother often bought little chicks which we kept in the house until they were big enough to take out to the chicken pen. We always had plenty of chicken when visitors arrived.

Mother would catch a couple of fryers and ring their necks. They would flop around for a while and then she would dip them in hot water to loosen the feathers. Plucking the feathers was a smelly job. Mother could quickly cut up and fry chicken for the crowds that we always had at our house. As each of the relatives came to California they always spent time at our house and most worked for the Steadman Brothers at the Ord Ranch.

The little house by the slough and the bigger house where Weemie lived were used by many of my family members later when they came to California. The big house is where the cook lived and there were tents for the workers. Nearby there was a smoke house and cook shack. Before Mr. Weems died Weemie's job was cooking and later my grandmother did this job.

The gentle hillside out from the smoke house was an Indian burial ground and lots of arrow heads could be found. This was a playground for all the cousins as they came to California. When Grandmama and

Leonard Anderson lived in the big house we visited often. There was a cellar to play in and outside we would walk to the slough. Many pictures were taken with the smoke house as a background because it was covered with climbing small pink roses.

When I was about six years old, we visited my grandmother and uncles that lived off and on in these two houses. That is where I learned to smoke. The kids would go to the slough behind the little house and swing on the grapevines. We used little pieces of the grapevine to smoke. They were thin and hollow so you could draw smoke through it. Just had to be careful not to suck a spark down your throat. I really didn't like this and I was glad when my cousin Louis Wayne Wilks moved to California in July, 1947. Louis Wayne didn't like to smoke so we found other things to do. He encouraged me to expand my talents. I learned to climb trees and I was brave when we were together. Mother had to get us out of the pig pen one day because we were riding the big sows. We had no idea how dangerous it was. The sows were mean when they had little piglets.

Ben Davis, Myrtle Anderson, Elbert Wilks
Uncle Sonny Anderson

**Grandmama Myrtle, Ben Davis, Benny Earl in
shadow and Louis Wayne Wilks**

The movies were a treat for the six Wilks cousins.
Left to Rt. John Wesley, Louis Wayne,
Vera Lou, LaTeresa Ann, Imogene, Benny Earl
We are going to the afternoon movie.

Daddy's brother Thurman had three kids. Benny Earl was John's age and LaTeresa Ann was Imogene's age. Louis Wayne was a year older than me and we were not gender matched, but I got the best friend out of the deal. It was a short time because I was just eight years old when Louis Wayne died. With no playmate I had to join the other cousins. This meant I had to smoke. They said I might tell on them if I didn't smoke. By the time I was eight they had graduated from smoking grapevines to cigarettes. So at age eight I became a smoker. Two years later, Irene Davis the cousin that moved to Biggs from Colorado was my age and in my class so we were partners. We spent lots of time walking down the railroad tracks and always had cigarettes we stole from her mother.

When Wayne died I had no idea that he was sick enough to die. I knew that he didn't feel good sometimes and he couldn't eat much. His mother Pauline was always yelling at him about not eating enough.

One day I was at his house and he went in to ask for a sandwich. His mother yelled at him for not eating when she cooked his lunch. He certainly didn't feel like eating then. My folks had taken him to see Dr. Frank I. O'Neill in Oroville, but he never was able to make a diagnosis of the problem. Actually, there was nothing that they could do since he didn't have a functioning pituitary gland. The Pituitary Gland is the major endocrine gland that controls growth and development. Wayne was one of the oldest to have this condition.

In the night in October 1948, Daddy and Mother took Wayne and his parents to the hospital in Oroville. Louis Wayne's last comment on the way over was for my Dad to slow down. He said, "Please tell Uncle Elbert to slow down." The motion of the car was too much for him.

The next morning I knew nothing of the activity of the night before so I went to school as usual. Mrs. Alexander was my teacher and I thought she couldn't remember what she had taught the day before. She was teaching division and every day she would go over the same thing. I didn't realize until I became a teacher that you do have to repeat the process so all the students will get it. When the day was over I rode home on the school bus and went skipping up to the back door. There were lots of cars in the yard, but that wasn't different enough for me to think anything was wrong. Aunt Mary met me about half way to the back door and told me, "Honey, Louis Wayne passed away."

I had no response because I didn't know what 'passed away' meant. I knew something was wrong when I opened the back door because Wayne's mother was in my Mom and Dad's room and she was bellowing like a cow. I asked mother, "What is wrong with her?"

Mother told me, "She is so upset because Louis Wayne died." I had a response to this comment, "Why? She didn't like him. She was mean to him."

Mother tried to convince me that Pauline loved him and she was truly grieving for him. I shook loose from Mother's hands that were on my shoulders and went into the dining room. I was just standing there starting to cry and in my eight year old wisdom I decided that if I really loved him I would not cry because I could hear how his mother was crying like a sick cow and I knew she didn't love him.

This confusion of love, loss, and expression of feeling has plagued me all my life. It was reinforced often. In fact at Wayne's funeral I sat outside the family room with my sister Imogene. We could see past the curtain and the whole room of people were crying. Even my uncle Sonny had been shipped home from the Navy to sit in the family room and was crying and blowing his nose. I could still hear Pauline howling and crying.

I sat there in excruciating pain and swallowed my tears. Later, Mother took me to Louis Wayne's grave after his stone was in place and I was angry all over again when I saw that his mother had changed his name. She put Wayne L. Wilks on his stone. The anger and hate that I had for his mother influenced every part of my life.

The fun part of the following years were the parties that we had each weekend. Don had married Aunt Billie and she had a precious little girl Linda Kay. Soon they had Jerry Don and I got to carry him around. Aunt Billie would always make fudge when she came. We usually ended up licking the spoons because it rarely set like real fudge. In 1948, the same year that Louis Wayne died, Imogene got a new bicycle and the family got a new phonograph. We had no music in the house except Granddad Taylor's radio for the Grand Ole Opry. We had very few records, but I wore out the ones I liked. 'House of Blue Lights' I loved because Aunt Billie had taught us to JitterBug to that record.

Aunt Billie could play chop sticks on the piano and Aunt Mary could play 'Sentimental Journey' by ear. Aunt Mary was like one of us kids when it was time to stop at the East Gridley Store and get a milkshake. She would take us places in their Model A with the rumble seat. Usually she took us to her house on Chester and Amy Hoar's place. The turn to Aunt Mary's house was off Larkin Road just north of our first little house. She would get us to help with her house cleaning and outside chores and then off to get an ice cream. Mother enjoyed the baby-sitting so she could get her own things done.

I wasn't old enough for 4-H, but I got to go with Imogene to every meeting. Lorene Kenneck was the sewing leader and she became a close friend of mine because she paid attention to me. Her husband Roy and Daddy became good friends because of their instant connection. When they first met they knew that each had done time. Something in the lingo!! Their daughter Joy May was a school friend and 4-H friend of Imogene's. About the same time that Imogene got her new bike, the Kenneck's had a complete auction at their house and moved to Southern California. Lorene Kenneck gave me Joy May's bicycle and I was so delighted to have my own bike. Imogene would let me ride hers some, but I didn't like to beg. I still have the scar from learning to ride the bicycle. This was a fun activity and Mother and Daddy joined us out on the road riding the bicycles.

Evening drives were part of our fun because Daddy always had someone to see about a job or equipment or whatever. He would talk and we often had to wait way too long. One afternoon he came home early and was excited to show us Jamaican people. One of the peach farmers had brought in a load of Jamaicans to pick the crop of ripe peaches. Daddy was talking a mile a minute and I didn't know why he was making such a big deal. He was telling us to look at how slow they move. Even going up the ladder every move is in a slow, syncopated rhythm. Also look at the flat noses. It was years later that I learned why Daddy was so interested in the Jamaicans. He had worked with the Jamaicans on the banana boat loaded with SUGAR that he helped bring into New Orleans for Al Capone's operation. Capone and Daddy had been cell neighbors when he was in Atlanta, Georgia, so he had the directions and signal to get in the door of the Speak Easy spots in New Orleans. Capone was moved from Atlanta, Georgia, to Alcatraz August 19, 1934, but he continued directing his business on the outside.

Ben Davis, my paternal grandmother's half-brother, married Mary Evelyn Bryan in Cooper, Texas, in November, 1938. Ben and Mary came to California from Sulphur Springs, Texas in 1947 soon after Thurman and Pauline Wilks. They stayed at our house when they first arrived, but it didn't take long for my Mom and Dad to help them get started.

Uncle Ben went to work for the Steadman's on the Ord Ranch and Aunt Mary was hired at the telephone office in Gridley. Mother made some gathered skirts for her to wear to her new job. She was so naive that she told them that she had to go back to Texas for her furniture and would be back after Christmas. She showed up for work in January, 1948. They had not saved the position for her, but another operator, Ethel Corcoran, retired so Aunt Mary started her career as a telephone operator. She has enough stories to write her own book. Gridley soon went dial and Aunt Mary moved to the Oroville office. This is about the same time that we had a phone installed at the ranch in the early 1950's. Now, Daddy was able to make some of his contacts on the phone.

Originally, Ben and Mary lived on the Smith Ranch on Hiway 99 owned by Mrs. Doty. This is the ranch that had nectarines and fruit that Daddy packed for the market.

Daddy made contact with Vince DaMassa in San Francisco and he packed fruit for the San Francisco Farmers Market. This came in handy when the Libby Cannery went on strike with peaches ripe in the field. My Dad had his peaches on the way to San Francisco to the fresh fruit market.

Occasionally, one of us kids would get to ride in the truck to the city. I remember the roar of the motor in the old surplus army truck as Daddy pulled the hills on Hiway 40 when it was a two lane road. Now it is a freeway called Interstate 80. It was already four lanes and the big dip was taken out when I was driving to College at Berkeley in 1958-9. One time that John rode with Daddy, they had the load too high and they crashed going under an underpass that was too low. John had a big lip from the accident. Earlier Daddy had shown John the picture of the advertisement for Ben Davis overalls. It was a gorilla dressed in the overalls and Daddy made a joke about his Uncle Ben Davis that was bringing an army surplus truck to California. When Ben arrived John looked long and hard at him and then said to Daddy, "He doesn't look like his picture."

Thurman, my Dad's only full blood brother, and his wife Pauline had come the month before and my Dad had gone into partnership with Thurman. Wilks Brothers, Route 1, Box 45, Biggs, California.

They leased orchards and some land for raising tomatoes. Thurman was so jealous of Ben that Daddy couldn't have him work for them. Thurman was a drinker also and the tomato rows were crooked as a snake with him driving. It was quite a drain on the income since Thurman and Pauline only had another old army surplus truck to put into the partnership.

As the relatives came to California they were busy with jobs mainly for the Steadman brothers. Daddy's brother had joined him in business on the farm. Aunt Mary was a telephone operator and her husband Ben Davis was working on the Ord Ranch with his brothers Jeff and Roy.

May 10, 1950, my Uncle Roy Davis was killed in an accident at work. Ben was driving tractor pulling a spray rig with Roy in a tower spraying the trees. Ben pulled too close to a high line wire and Roy was electrocuted. Roy had married Pauline's sister Bingo and she did the crying thing. Aunt Mary was supportive to her husband Ben because he was devastated knowing that he was responsible for Roy's death.

I was almost ten years old and stayed very detached from the trauma. I knew that there was something wrong with the marriage to Bingo and later I learned that Roy was drunk when he married her and not too pleased when he sobered up and found he was married. Roy and Jeff were the two uncles that were still practicing alcoholics. They didn't drink all the time, but they would go on binges and it could be months before they returned to work and life.

Roy was kind and soft spoken. He had lived with us off and on when we first got to California. The off time was when he was on a binge because Mother and Dad wouldn't let him stay there when he was drunk. Roy is buried in the Gridley-Biggs Cemetery at the opposite end of the block of six graves bought for Louis Wayne. Roy's death and funeral brought up all the hurt and loss of my cousin and playmate less than two years before.

My grandmother Myrtle and her husband Leonard Anderson lived on Larkin Road near the bridge that goes nowhere. The bridge has been removed, but we used it to play around when we stayed at

Grandmama's house. There was a big sycamore tree in the front yard. Without air-conditioning the men Leonard, Jeff, Ben, Daddy, Thurman could always be found sitting in a circle under the shade tree. One day I was running from the bridge that goes nowhere to Grandmama's house. As I quickly passed the circle of men under the shade tree I overheard Leonard Anderson say, "And look at us now all out here **working**."

I was ten years old and traveling fast, but I knew that the intonation did not fit the statement. They were sitting doing nothing and the statement was so incongruent that I never forgot it. Years later I found out that he was talking about the whole clan being in California and they all had jobs instead of making moonshine.

My Dad had facilitated the move of each of the families and Steadman's gave them a job when they arrived in Gridley. Granddad still worked for Steadman's. Starting in 1950 Ernie Steadman carried the casket at each of the Wilks and Davis funerals.

Shortly after Roy's accident Ben and Mary went to Pinal County, Arizona. William L. Speed (Speedy) who later married Imogene was in Eloy, Arizona. Eloy was still a real Old West town and when we drove through in 1948 it still had board sidewalks. Speedy had influence with Sheriff Earley so he helped him to hire cooperating deputies. Leo Davis was already there and soon they asked Ben to come over. Speedy brokered the deal to get the job. Ben had to pay money and he didn't have to go through a background check, thank goodness, because Ben had done his time in prison during the depression. Ben was a well liked deputy and served under two different sheriffs.

The way I met many relatives is when they came to work for my Dad. Pete Taylor came one summer because Daddy needed extra help in the orchards. Pete had witnessed my Dad's temper when he was irritated about problems that always came up. Pete had a major accident in the orchard and dumped a load of peaches trying to make a corner too close. He was in a dither about how he was going to tell Bert. Mother assured him it would be okay. When the tragedy had already happened Bert just went to work thinking of a way to correct it. He just smiled and said, "I guess you tried that one a little too fast."

Summer of 1952, I was helping pack tomatoes for the San Francisco market. Daddy had stayed in touch with Vince DaMassa and he often sent early packed peaches or tomatoes to San Francisco Farmers Market. It was too early to pick the tomatoes for the cannery, but Daddy didn't let a nickel slip by. He was packing the pinks for Vince. It was fun to pack tomatoes because they didn't have fuzz like the peaches. You had to be sure to keep the sizes even so they fit perfectly in the L.A. lug.

I was packing tomatoes when I learned that mother was going to have a baby. Big surprise, I thought she was too old for that business, but it was for real. They made a deal with Aunt Mary and Uncle Ben. If it were a girl she was to be named Mary and a boy would be named Ben. This is the same fall that Daddy visited Arthur Davis in Sulphur Springs, Texas, and Ben and Mary in Arizona. Daddy brought back hand tooled leather four inch platform high heels. He bought them on a side trip to Old Mexico. Mother couldn't begin to wear them because she was so big with Mary Kay. Aunt Mary was excited when she heard it was A GIRL born December 27, 1952. My little sister was named Mary Kay Wilks after our Aunt Mary.

The Wilks Brothers partnership was terrible. My grandmother and Pauline were big talkers and gossip creators. Something was always being stirred up and my Dad knew that he had to break the partnership. When they went to work on him to fire Mother's brother Uncle Lee, because of lies they were telling on Lee, Mother told Daddy it was time to make the break. He got the split made at quite a financial loss for our family.

Mother was so thankful when the split was complete and Daddy had new land leased with corn planted and another area for tomatoes. Daddy also had the first corn picker to come into the area ordered. He had bought a new big truck from S.S. Hinaman and Son Ford Garage in Gridley. Daddy was still milking cows and Mother had laying hens and a big garden.

June 10, 1954, I graduated from Biggs Elementary School. I was nervous because I had to speak. I was just presenting the gift to our teacher Mr. Buchla. I was upset about more than the presentation before we walked on stage because I knew my Dad wasn't there. He was late for my graduation.

Daddy did get to the graduation, but at the dance afterward I knew he had been drinking. I was really mad at him. Later, I found out that he was using the whiskey for pain and he had a heart attack before my graduation. Days later he went to the hospital. I visited him and he thought he was getting better. He was writing a letter to Ben and Mary since they were in Arizona at this time. He told them that he thought he was dying, but now he felt better and guessed he was going to make it. The orderly told mother that he was listening to Bert tell a joke when he grabbed his chest and died.

June 17, 1954, Mother received a phone call from the hospital. She was so shocked that she hung up on them. I don't remember much about the next few days. Mother had to make calls and Mrs. Rocha on the party line would not get off and acted like mother was lying when she said she needed the phone for death messages. Later, after the news was out, she brought a box of doughnuts to the family and apologized.

Mother was in shock for weeks. Her face had a frozen smile and she talked to the hundreds of people that came to the house with food and words of sympathy. John was supposed to go to a little league game. I did the ironing because it was therapeutic. I was an observer and I couldn't understand why everyone talked about how young my dad was because at thirteen I didn't realize forty-two is young. I made it through the funeral without crying. In private much later I did shed a few tears.

The time of the year made it necessary for Mother to quickly take over the farming operation. Peaches were getting ripe, a new truck to pay for, corn picker to take delivery on, tomatoes to be cared for, spaying jobs to fill.

My mother had plenty to deal with and then there was Grandmama Myrtle and Uncle Thurman out in the community taking jobs away from Mother. They told people that they were taking care of Bert's jobs. And they along with others were walking into the garage and barn and taking Daddy's tools. Mother had to sell the cows because she got a bad kick the first time she tried to milk the cows.

Salvador, the Mexican worker that lived on our place, told Mother that he had to go back to Mexico because it wasn't proper for him to work for a woman. Luckily, he was there for about a month because we were home alone when a child predator came to the house. He was pushing his way into the house and up to no good. Salvador came up to the main house and sent him on his way.

Mother's brother Lee told her that Bert had talked to him before he went to the hospital and asked him to help mother when she picked up the corn picker. Then when she went to get the insurance on the truck she found out that Bert had checked with Mr. Hinaman before his death to be sure that the death benefit was on the truck insurance. That made it hard for Mr. Hinaman to tell mother that they had denied the death benefit on the truck because it was a commercial vehicle. Hardships to say the least.

Mary Kay was just eighteen months old and Imogene took care of her. When school started Katie rode with Mother and Imogene came home early from school to help. We saw very little of Mother because she would usually go to work before we woke up in the morning and didn't get home until bedtime. She became known as the 'Lady Farmer' of Butte County.

The first year after a death is so difficult. My life had been turned upside down again. Some things continued such as school, 4-H, and holidays. Our neighbors and 4-H leaders Orwin and Carma Pryde invited us for Thanksgiving Dinner. It was so strange not to have all the clan for Thanksgiving. Christmas we had very few presents and not much joy. Daddy was the one that made the holidays big events.

Aunt Mary and Uncle Ben were living in Arizona where Ben was a Deputy Sheriff and Mary was the Chief Operator in Coolidge. They came for Daddy's funeral and planned their vacation the next year for May 12, 1955, so they could come and see the family. They packed into the night and neither would look at the clock because they were superstitious about leaving on their vacation on the 13th. This is less than eleven months since Daddy's death. From this visit I remember going for a ride in their new, red and white, Crown Victoria Ford and Ben was driving. We just went a short distance and Ben turned around at Pasquini's on Hiway 99E. Ben took us back home because he needed the 'soda'. Baking soda was what he used for indigestion.

On the return trip to Arizona the next day Ben and Mary stopped in Beaumont, California, to spend the night. Aunt Mary knew that Ben was not feeling well because they had come upon an accident and he wanted to stop and help with the traffic control, but he didn't feel well enough. He then stopped for some 7-up and Pepto Bismol.

Ben walked into the motel room in Beaumont, California, carrying the overnight case. Mary was behind him when he collapsed on the floor. Mary screamed and got help. When the doctors got there she was given sedatives and they made a few necessary calls to get people there to help her. Leo and Vera Davis came from Arizona and many from the Sheriff's Department came to Gridley for the funeral. It was Sonny Anderson that rode the train with Ben's body.

Just eleven months after Daddy's funeral we got the news that Ben was dead May 22, 1955. Aunt Mary came to our house and she was delirious with grief and overdosed on sedatives. I have little memory of the events that followed. My brother John was beating his pillow with anger and grief. He had lost his Dad, his goat had died and now his favorite Uncle Ben.

My sister graduated from High School a few days later. She had scholarships and planned to go to U.C. Davis. Instead she went to be with Aunt Mary in Arizona. While in Arizona, Imogene met and later married Speedy. Aunt Mary got a transfer to Marysville telephone office. She rented an apartment in Maryville and soon bought a house in Olivehurst, California.

The next year was a blur. Aunt Mary met many people in Marysville and at Beale Air Force Base. She brought many to see us and I visited her also. It was a treat to stay at her house because I could openly smoke there. My smokes at home were hidden, but I did smoke regularly now. My Uncle Lee tried to get me to quit. One day he had me figure how much money I would spend on cigarettes over forty years. Then I was paying twenty-five cents a pack in the machine in front of the Grocery store. I wasn't old enough to buy them at the counter, but I was smoking too much to keep stealing them. I did smoke for over forty years, but I paid a lot more than twenty-five cents a pack. I have to agree with Mark Twain, "It is easy to quit, I've done it hundreds of times." But also I had to agree with Mark Twain in that I didn't want to die a 'Moral Pauper' without a vice to throw overboard in case I got sick.

During the summers I worked in the peach orchards. I drove the Ford tractor pulling a trailer to distribute the boxes to each set of four trees. I learned to drive the Model A truck down the rows while the guys were loading the lugs of picked peaches. After Imogene married I had her job of checking boxes. That is where you count how many boxes each picker has picked and punch a card to tell Mother how much to pay them.

In April of 1956, Mother married Fred Stanley Wilson. Fred knew mother when she and Daddy had the big garden at the first little house. Now he had the hauling contract at Libby Cannery so he hired Mother's new truck that she had to pay for after Daddy's death. Mother continued the farming, but she was able to let the leased land go and just take care of the peaches at home. She helped Fred at the cannery. Her spot was in the scale house taking orders, running errands and keeping books.

I turned sixteen in August so I could go to work in the cafeteria at the cannery. Life had changed but I thought I was grown and did take charge of my life meeting all the troubles and hardships with the 'Can Do' attitude. Unfortunately, my early experiences made me an observer of life rather than a full participant. I don't think my Granddad was responsible for me being such an observer of life but he was a stoic person and he had been the responsible one in his family at a very young age when his father died. Then his brothers and little girl died in New Mexico and shortly after his wife died in 1918 his two sisters died just months apart. It was difficult for me to fully participate in life because I was hurt often by death or separation so I found it easier to keep my feelings protected.

I graduated from Biggs High School as Valedictorian. It was easy to study. My classmates had no idea the pain that I was suffering. I had lost my cousin/playmate at age 8, my Uncle Roy died before I was 10, my father died when I was 13, Uncle Ben when I was 14 and I lost the love of my life when I was 17. I had my first daughter by a man that was totally unavailable. Victoriano Acebo was married and not mine to have. Two years later I married Al Turner an intelligent, good man who was emotionally unavailable. We made a pact when we got married to never speak of love. He had been hurt emotionally and found it difficult to love. He had his first and only experience with love when our daughter Jennifer was born. He just loved her and once the bond was there he never lost it. We divorced after twenty-three years of marriage because I knew what love was and I couldn't live without it any longer. Al and I had a productive marriage. We were a good team. I was always out looking for projects and property. If Al agreed to a project he was a finisher so he built a house for the family on Clay Station Rd in Herald and developed property on Sand Ridge Road near Plymouth, California. We also had two terrific children, Jennifer Lee and Erik Albert. Al also adopted my first born so she was raised Valorie Lynn Turner.

**My kids Erik Albert Turner, Jennifer Lee
Turner Herting, Valorie Lynn Turner
taken August 14, 2010**

The many losses in my life helped set my philosophy of life. 'Plan as if you will live to be 110 and live each day as if it is your last.' You will be kind and helpful and never intentionally hurt anyone if you consider this to be your last day.

www.ingramcontent.com/pod-product-compliance
Lightning Source LLC
Chambersburg PA
CBHW020257290526
45784CB00003B/1278